# A FRENCH RENAISSANCE?

## Note from the author

This is a true story based on real-life events. However, the names of some people and places have been changed in order to preserve the anonymity of those involved who may not wish to be identified.

# A FRENCH RENAISSANCE?

*An Irish Family Moves to France*

## Eamon O'Hara

ORPEN PRESS

Published by
Orpen Press
Lonsdale House
Avoca Avenue
Blackrock
Co. Dublin
Ireland

e-mail: info@orpenpress.com
www.orpenpress.com

Paperback ISBN 978-1-909895-38-6
ePub ISBN 978-1-909895-40-9
Kindle ISBN 978-1-909895-41-6
PDF ISBN 978-1-909895-42-3

Printed in Dublin by SPRINT-print Ltd.

*Dedicated to my parents, Michael and Joan*

## About the Author

Eamon O'Hara is a freelance writer, entrepreneur and European policy specialist. A native of Carlow in Ireland, he co-founded Carlow Brewing Company (O'Hara's Brewery) with his brother in 1996. In 2001, he moved to Brussels to work in European affairs and recently co-founded ECOLISE, a European network to support local action on climate change and sustainability. He currently lives with his wife and children in southwest France, where they run a successful tourism business.

www.eamonohara.com

# Acknowledgements

The first people I have to thank are my fellow adventurers: Tanya, my wife, partner in crime and soul mate, without whom no journey would be the same; and our two children, Ned and Astrid, who were the inspiration for our move to France and who continue to inspire every aspect of our lives – three special people with whom I feel very privileged to be able to share my life.

A special thanks also to Ailbhe, Eileen and all the team at Orpen Press for giving me this opportunity, and for their commitment, dedication and professionalism. I am especially grateful to Eileen for her intelligent and insightful suggestions and editorial input.

I am grateful also to the many other people who helped and supported me throughout the writing process, in particular Deirdre O'Neill, Antonia Hart and my parents-in-law, Victor and Rachel Treacy.

Finally, I take this opportunity to thank my family and friends for their unwavering support, tolerance and good humour. To my brothers, Seamus and Michael, my sisters, Fiona and Siobhán, to all the old crew from Bagenalstown, and to my other good friends in Ireland, Belgium, France and elsewhere; thank you!

# Contents

Preface .................................................................................. xi

Introduction ........................................................................ 1

1  The Call that Changed Our Lives ............................ 9
2  A Coup de Coeur ......................................................... 18
3  A Second Chance ........................................................ 33
4  Happy Monday ........................................................... 46
5  Blue Tuesday ............................................................... 51
6  Bah Humbug ................................................................ 59
7  Beers and Tears .......................................................... 62
8  The New Life ............................................................... 72
9  Strangers in a Strange Land .................................... 86
10  The Cowboy Architect .............................................. 101
11  Living the Green Dream ........................................... 118
12  Tensions Rising .......................................................... 132
13  The Summer of Discontent ...................................... 149
14  Half-Baked .................................................................. 162
15  Easy in Autumn ......................................................... 171
16  A White Christmas .................................................... 179
17  A Man Needs a Tractor ............................................ 186
18  Take Two ...................................................................... 194
19  Taking Stock ............................................................... 200

Epilogue ............................................................................... 206

# Preface

The inspiration to write this book came to me one day as I stood on the side of the street in Brussels watching my car swinging through the air, having been lifted by a crane from a large hole in the ground. This was just a few hours before we were due to sign the contract on the sale of our house, and the day before we were supposed to make a long anticipated move to the south of France. It was a bizarre moment, which had been proceeded by a number of other strange and unexpected events, and as the small group of bystanders who gathered to watch this unusual spectacle oohed and aahed in tandem with the oscillations of the car, it suddenly dawned on me that this move we were about to undertake was going to be no ordinary experience.

In moving to France we were pushing the boundaries, at least our own boundaries, which was leading to all kinds of weird and sometimes wonderful happenings, and I had the feeling that I should try to document it. From then on I began keeping a diary and, as it happened, these early incidents turned out to be only the tip of the iceberg and paled into insignificance in comparison to what would unfold over the following months, as we sought to settle into our new home and our new life in rural France.

During this period, there were high points and low points. There were times when we celebrated the move and times when we questioned and even cursed it. Throughout, however, I was continually struck by the keen interest of friends, colleagues and acquaintances in our progress – and not just on a superficial level, but often in the specific details. There was a real curiosity about what we were doing, how we had made it happen and how it was working out. It felt like we were guinea pigs, like we were testing the waters for their own possible move to rural France. I decided, therefore, to turn my diary into a book that would try to satisfy this curiosity, giving a blow-by-blow account of the move, while also sharing the experiences and lessons we learned along the way. In writing this book I have tried to be as honest and frank as possible and as you read on one thing you will discover, as we did, is that moving to the south of France has been nothing like we expected.

We started out with romantic notions of a leisurely family life in the French countryside but the reality has been completely different. That is not to say it has been all bad, which is not the case. It has just been different: some of the things we expected and hoped for we have struggled with, while other things we didn't even contemplate have now become important and treasured aspects of our lives. Along the way, we have grown and matured as a family and as individuals. We have learned some valuable lessons about life, which apply not just in rural France but anywhere people seek to change their lives for the better. Ultimately, this is a book about people, place and relationships and how these impact on our lives and our sense of who we are and what we do.

This book covers the period from the later stages of our property search right up to the end of our second year in France. This was a crucial period in terms of the move, from the excitement of finding the property of our dreams through to the challenges we encountered in trying to settle into our new life in a new community. At the end of the book I take the story right up to the present, with an update on our current situation and how we feel about the move four years on.

I hope you find our story enjoyable and useful, but also inspirational. Having been through this experience, I am convinced more than ever that life change is a realistic goal for anyone who desires it. I hope this book will help you on this journey and, even if it doesn't inspire you to move to rural France, I am certain it will provide some useful insights into how you can change your life for the better. In the words of George Eliot, 'It is never too late to be who you might have been.'

# Introduction

Somewhere in back of my mind, my subconscious has been busy for many years, creating a picture of what might be an idyllic lifestyle. Every now and then, during those dreamy moments between sleep and wake, I would get a glimpse of it. It seemed attractive, but always remote and somewhat fictional. In this picture, I would relocate with my family to somewhere in the French countryside to pursue my dream of being a writer. We would live in an old French château or farmhouse, full of character, with a big old fireplace, lots of oak beams, and full-length French windows leading out onto a shaded terrace. There, my wife Tanya and I would sit with our chilled glasses of rosé, surveying the gardens, the orchard and the 20 or so acres of land that lay beyond, while I pondered the words I had just penned.

The climate would be dry and sunny, but not too hot – somewhere in the southwest of France perhaps. Here, in this French idyll, we would live life at our own pace; rising early, cycling or walking to the village for fresh bread and croissants, and then back to enjoy a leisurely breakfast in the garden, basking in the morning sun. Following breakfast, I would retreat to my characterful office, where I would give life to the ideas and stories I had been carrying around in my head all my life. At midday, I would re-join my family and we would dine on the finest of fresh food from the garden or local markets. This would be followed by another hour or two of writing, or perhaps a siesta if I felt the need. Later in the afternoon, we would work together in the garden or on the land, or some days we might just laze by the pool or take off to explore some of the many hidden gems in this beautiful part of France.

In addition to a burgeoning vegetable garden and orchard, we would also have our own chickens, pigs and some cattle, making us practically self-sufficient in terms of food. An extensive area of woodland would also provide enough fuel for heating and an array of solar panels would cater for all our electricity needs.

You could call it the good life, and it does all sound a bit idyllic, but it's funny how things that get lodged in the back of your mind one day end up staring you in the face. And here I am, and here we are, now the proud owners of the aforementioned old characterful château, with 40 acres of land (not 20!), the vegetable garden, the orchard, and even a swimming pool and an old barn, part of which has been converted into a gîte (a rural holiday rental, usually in a traditional building).

Where did it all go right, you might ask? Well, actually, it didn't all go right. Firstly, it didn't happen overnight. The idea that was lodged in the back of my mind was there for quite a long time and, for financial and other reasons, it took many years and considerable effort to make it a reality. In fact, for a while I put it out of my mind altogether, or so I thought, as it just didn't seem realistic, but something inside my subconscious just wouldn't let it lie and kept steering me in this direction. Looking back now, some of the questionable life decisions I made over the years suddenly make perfect sense in terms of ultimately moving to France. It was the same for Tanya. Like me, she also dreamed about such a move for many years, but she didn't really believe it would ever happen, as there just seemed to be too many hurdles to overcome.

Secondly – and I'm sure this applies to more or less everyone who realises certain plans or ambitions in their lives – the reality is nothing like the dream. In saying that, I don't mean it's not worth it, but what you never seem to visualise in the dream are the challenges and sacrifices that have to be made along the way, or the cracks behind the sometimes very alluring façade; how difficult it can be to find your beautiful old stone farmhouse, and, when you do find it, how difficult it might be to heat it in winter, or how much work is involved in maintaining 40 acres and a swimming pool. And the neighbours rarely get a look in, at least in my dreams, especially the devious ones.

Dreams are just dreams, and although we can strive to make them a reality, things never turn out exactly as we imagine. But this is not necessarily such a bad thing, and if our move to France has taught me anything it's that almost realising a dream is probably a more realistic prospect and maybe not such a bad outcome in the end.

§

Tanya and I originally left Ireland in 2001. The country was in the middle of an economic boom – so not the most obvious time to up sticks and leave – but economic booms mean different things to different people and, for us, the distant fields still held a greater allure. At the time, we lived in Dublin (although we are originally from the south-east of the country) so we partly blamed the traffic congestion, the lengthy commutes to work, the long walks home from the city centre on Saturday nights because we couldn't get a taxi, the spiralling property prices, and the many other inconveniences of a country in the thrall of an economic explosion. These were certainly contributory factors, but they weren't the whole story. Ireland is a small and some-times claustrophobic country, and, for us, going abroad was never just about economics. It was also a chance to reinvent ourselves, to broaden our horizons and to dis-cover new things about ourselves and the world. So when an opportunity to move to Brussels came along, we were ready for a change.

It was exciting to have the chance to live abroad and, given that I had been working on a European programme in Ireland, Brussels had an added appeal. For the first year abroad, maybe more, it felt like we were tourists; everything was new and different, and there always seemed to be something more to discover. Our lifestyle was also a lot easier than it had been in Dublin. We could afford a nice house, in a nice location, there was no traffic congestion, no taxi problems, lots of nice places to socialise; the quality of life was just better. Of course, we missed our friends and family, but at just over an hour's flight from Dublin, we always had a steady stream of visitors, and we made some good friends in Brussels, which is a melting pot of different nationalities.

Our stay in Belgium was meant to be short, possibly a year, but by the end of the first year, it still felt like we had just arrived and we weren't ready to return to Ireland. During our second year in Belgium we got married. We had a civil ceremony in Schaerbeek Town Hall, a spectacular building in the heart of the city, with about thirty invited guests. It was perfect, and exactly as we wanted it. After a few more years abroad, the prospect of returning to Ireland seemed to become more and more remote. Somehow, it felt like our journey was onwards rather than backwards.

There is always a conflict when you live abroad: on the one hand, you miss your family and friends and the chance to share your everyday life with them, and there's also the pull of the familiar and of the place that still defines a large part of who you are. On the other hand, there's the fear of getting drawn back into a life that you voluntarily left behind, and the desire to keep the adventure alive. It's an odd feeling of being enticed and repelled at the same time. The perfect manifestation of this is the pub, which I often tell people is one of the things I miss most about Ireland – being able to casually meet up with people for a chat and a few drinks.

At the same time, drinking, and the tendency in Ireland to overdo it, is one of the reasons I'm glad to be living abroad.

In July 2006 our first child, Ned, was born in Brussels. Ned's arrival opened a new chapter in our lives, which might never have happened if we had stayed in Ireland. We didn't know it before we emigrated, but Brussels is home to one of the world's top IVF clinics and if not for this, chances are we would never have been able to have children. In October 2008 our second child, Astrid, was born. We were overjoyed. After six years and many IVF attempts we had two beautiful, healthy children, and it changed our lives, completely.

Anyone who has children will understand how they become the centre of your world. All of a sudden, these small, precious little people are in your care and everything else takes second place. The things that were once the main focus of your life just seem less important – it's not that they don't matter anymore, but you just see them in a different light. This jolt to the system can also be the catalyst for some serious self-reflection. It certainly was in my case, and I became much more aware of my physical and mental wellbeing. I realised that I needed, and wanted, to be around for my children for as long as possible, and I wanted to be a happy dad, not a bitter or regretful one. So I found myself eating more healthily and exercising more, although I wasn't doing great in the sleep department. I also started to rethink my career. It wasn't that I didn't like my job, I just didn't see it as my life's work, as the thing that defined me. As a teenager and young adult, I had all kinds of other dreams and ambitions but somewhere along the way life had taken over. Getting a job and making money had become all-consuming, but I wanted to change that. Tanya too was reassessing her life. She had taken maternity leave from her job as a technical editor, but she had no real desire to go back. She wanted to be a hands-on mother and to pursue other things. Technical editing had been a means to an end, but her true interests lay elsewhere.

It was in this context that we started to give some serious consideration to the idea of moving to France. We both loved France. We holidayed there most years and we had often fantasised about starting a new life there. We had even made a pastime out of viewing properties for sale. Subconsciously, even though we had no concrete plan, I think we had been conditioning ourselves for such a move for many years, but when the children arrived it suddenly seemed like the right option. Somehow, Brussels didn't seem right for us anymore; we didn't feel rooted there, we didn't want our children to grow up in a city, and, if we stayed there, it didn't seem like we would ever have the time or space to pursue our real interests. France was going to be our chance to start a new life, a life that would better respond to our needs as a family and as individuals. The life we had dreamed about for years was suddenly becoming a realistic prospect. And so began our journey, a journey that has had more than its fair share of ups and downs, and one that carried with it the weight of high expectations.

## Another Life

The first question many people ask me when they hear about our move to France is, why? Why did you turn your back on a good job, a nice house and an easy urban lifestyle to embrace the unknown in the depths of rural France? It's a fair question, but usually when people ask me this I can tell that they already know the answer, and are simply looking for me to confirm what they already suspect.

For some people, it's a chance to raise a topic that they don't always feel free to talk about – as if it's some kind of taboo to desire something different to the life you have. Pinning your colours to the mast has a way of winning the confidence of people who latently or secretly share your views, and I was surprised how many people opened up to me on this. Clearly, many people are disillusioned with their current lifestyle: exhausted and unfulfilled by their work, confused about where their lives are heading, not having enough time or energy for family, friends or personal interests, and generally unhappy with the pressures and expectations of modern society. There are many people who feel trapped and powerless to change this situation. The fear of failure, financial insecurity, the loss of status, or being isolated can all provide a compelling case for grinning and bearing it – I know this from experience, as we also had these same fears, but we worked hard at minimising the risks and at reminding ourselves that we only had one life, and we eventually found ourselves in a situation where it just seemed like the time was right.

Minimising the risks was essential to helping us to overcome our concerns, and I expand on this throughout the book. Ultimately, however, we still had to trust in our own resourcefulness. We had to take the decision to move knowing that it was not completely foolproof; knowing that it could fail and that if it did, we would have to find a way to bounce back. We could, as some suggested, have waited until we were older and more financially secure, but we wanted to move while we were still young enough to build a new life, and while the children were young and better able to adjust and reap the benefits of growing up in a different country, with parents who had time and energy to devote to them.

In the end, deciding to move was actually the easy part. The more difficult decisions came later, when we had to sell our house, resign from our jobs, give up Ned's place in his new school, and spend our life's earnings on a property in a part of France we hardly knew. These were the decisions that really tested our resolve and commitment. Each one was difficult but every time we moved a step closer to our goal. If it hadn't felt right, then this would probably have been the point at which we abandoned the project, which would have been a major disappointment but perhaps not as disastrous as I might have thought at the time.

Moving to rural France is not for everyone and the important thing is to make a decision. One valuable lesson I have learned from our move is that life change is possible anywhere and once you decide where that is, you are already establishing a foundation for everything else. Family, community and a sense of place are essential ingredients for a happy life. Once you get these right, anything is possible.

# 1

# The Call that Changed Our Lives

Tuesday 6 October 2009 started out as a day much like any other. I woke about 7 a.m., showered, dressed and then tip-toed downstairs to avoid waking Tanya and the kids. I ate breakfast alone while watching the 24-hour news on TV. I then got my phone and my laptop, pulled on my jacket and left for work.

Outside in the Brussels street, a few other early risers were getting into their cars or making their way along the street, heads down, semi-oblivious to the world around them. What a shame I thought, as I shook myself down, double checking that I had all my essentials; whoever built these magnificent old townhouses, with their intricate art deco facades, would surely be disappointed that they no longer even raised the heads of passers-by.

As I walked through the Parc du Cinquantenaire that morning, I noticed that the trees had begun to change colour and there was already a wintry chill in the air. The vibrant greens of the exotic plane trees were giving way to sombre browns and yellows, and the bright blue mornings were beginning to fade into a more familiar grey. As autumn inevitably gave way to winter, I couldn't help feeling a sense of loss, of missed opportunity. It felt like a long way from the Lot Valley in the south of France, where we had spent two warm, sunny weeks in July. This now seemed like a distant memory as I trod the familiar route to work, and to a job from which I was feeling increasingly detached.

I had a meeting at the European Commission that morning. I was the manager of a team of specialists, or 'experts' in Brussels parlance, contracted by the Commission to assist in delivering aspects of one of its environmental programmes, and this was one of the monthly meetings with the officials involved. The bureaucracy of these meetings always left me feeling exhausted.

I got back to my office around 2.15 p.m. and I still hadn't gotten around to the tuna salad sandwich that was sitting on my desk when the phone rang. It was Tanya.

'Where have you been? I've been trying to get you for ages. You're not going to believe this …' she said, allowing some space for me to guess, but I had no idea where to start and I just didn't have the brain power anyway.

'Tell me.'

'Emily from Howard's phoned earlier. … She wanted to know if we were still interested in Laborie.'

Interesting news can be a bit like electric shock therapy for a clapped-out body, and all of sudden involuntary impulses were throwing me into a state of high alertness.

'What? Are you sure it's the same house?', I spluttered.

'Yes, I'm certain. She said the owner had contacted her yesterday to find out if we were still interested.'

'Wow. … Did she mention a price? Are they willing to accept our original offer?'

'She didn't say but she said if we were still interested we should try to go down for another viewing as soon as possible.'

I had a lot more questions but, frustratingly, Tanya didn't have much more information, so I hung up feeling excited but still intrigued. I could hardly believe we were back in the running for this property, especially as the offer we had made a few months earlier had been flatly rejected by the owners. It was the best possible news I could have wished for when I set out to work that morning.

And so began our life-changing journey, from hectic city centre living to, well, what we hoped would be a quieter, more balanced lifestyle in rural France.

§

The story really began about ten years earlier, in Ireland, when Tanya and I came up with a 'cunning plan', hatched over several pints of O'Hara's stout. We had just come back from holidays in France and our plan was that we were going to move there permanently, one day. Thinking about it now, this was more of an aspiration than a plan, as we had no idea where we were going to get the money or how we were going to make this happen, but we were determined.

Ever since then, we had been scouring websites looking for that idyllic French property, and on every holiday, which was always in France, we organised property viewings.

During this ten-year period, we travelled to France about fifteen times and, at a conservative estimate, I would say we had seen about 200 properties, spread right across southwest France, from Saint-Jean-de-Luz on the Atlantic coast to Saint-Guilhem-le-Désert near the Mediterranean coast, and north as far as the Corrèze and Dordogne. Some of these properties had been fantastic, but these were always a multiple of our budget. Unfortunately, everything falling within our budget was, well, below expectation.

Probably the closest contender in all of this period was a property near the medieval village of Cadouin, in the Dordogne. It was Easter 2009 and, having definitively decided to move to France at this stage, we had intensified our search, so this was just one of the properties we saw on this trip.

We were living in Brussels at this stage. Ned was two now and Astrid was only a couple of months old, so we had repeatedly stressed to the estate agent that we only wanted to look at real contenders – properties that met most of our criteria, which hadn't been the case on previous trips. She probably half got the message, which was a step forward. We saw some places that had some of what we wanted, but also a lot of what we didn't. By the afternoon of the third day we were tired, disillusioned and ready to call it a day, despite the fact that Caroline, the agent, had two more places left for us to visit.

As a last-ditch effort, she threw in a wild card, suggesting that instead of visiting these last two properties, which she acknowledged were more of the same, we could go and see a completely different property, one that she hadn't included on her list. Having spent almost three days with us, she said she felt that this was more suited to our needs. It sounded promising, even though we were nervous about getting our hopes up. The only problem was that it was a good hour's drive from our base in the village of Domme. Caroline was quite bullish, however, insisting that this could be the one: 'It has a very nice main house, four gîtes and a number of other outbuildings, lots of land, a beautiful garden. I really think it's what you're looking for', she insisted. 'And the village of Cadouin is really beautiful, with a well-known twelfth-century Cistercian abbey, a UNESCO World Heritage Site, which is also part of the famous pilgrim route to Santiago de Compostela [the Camino de Santiago].'

She was certainly pressing all the right buttons: Tanya and I loved walking, and we had hopes of walking the Camino ourselves one day, but we also had to consider the children. I really felt sorry for them during this trip, having to spend three days strapped in their car seats as we scurried from one property to the next. Mostly, they were as good as gold, but inevitably the schedule got the better of them and there were a few major blow-ups along the way. There were also plenty of nappy changes by the side of the road, in the boot of the car, in estate agents' offices and in a few other unlikely locations. This trip really brought it home to us that this was not something we could keep doing with kids.

We agreed to this one last visit with Caroline, but after that we would have a serious rethink. Caroline set off in her own car, with us in hot pursuit. Before going to the property, she took us to see the village of Cadouin, which was a smart move on her part. It's a really beautiful place, and in the evening sun it had an almost magical allure. Could this be the one, we mused, as we drove on to the stereo sound of two small and very reluctant junior house hunters.

My first impressions were not good. It was unremarkable – big, rectangular and lacking any real character. Inside, things did improve. There was a nice big old fireplace, a lovely oak staircase leading from the living room up to the first floor, and some really nice bedrooms upstairs, two of which had generous-sized balconies, which I really liked. But, like most of the properties we viewed in France, there were also some real oddities. All of the north-facing windows, for example, had been closed up. And I don't mean with curtains or wooden shutters – they had been built up with bricks and mortar. This left the house very dark and also gave it an eerie feeling. Caroline said it was to keep out the cold in winter, but it gave me the willies.

For me, the property had more bad points than good. Having said that, it was probably the best of all the properties we had seen in France up to this point and we were running out of steam, which wasn't helped by the fact that we were now dragging two small children along on every visit. So, despite its faults, I wasn't ruling it out.

Tanya, on the other hand, loved the place. The interior of the main house had cast a spell on her and she had been completely charmed by the village. Maybe there was also an element of being ground down by all the visits and the disappointments, but, whatever the reasons, she seemed certain that this was the one for her.

We drove back to Domme in relative silence that evening; I think we were all a bit war-weary and Tanya and I just didn't have the energy to confront our differences of option. It was only when we hit the motorway on the way home to Brussels the next morning that we felt ready to share our thoughts.

Despite three days of intensive property hunting, the discussion was largely confined to one property, which was disappointing. I think it was partly our own fault – for relying too much on the internet and not spending enough time in the area, but there also seemed to be a real lack of nice properties for sale. It was frustrating, as there are many really lovely properties in France, and we saw lots of them en route as we dragged ourselves from one crumbling shack to the next. But the reality is that most of these properties are not for sale, and, if they are, they're snapped up quickly and usually at a significant premium.

The asking price for the property in Cadouin was €560,000. I thought we would probably get it for around €500,000, but we would still need to spend a lot of money on the main house and quite a lot on the outbuildings. In all, allowing for tax and fees of about 12 per cent, I estimated that we would need a minimum budget of €650,000. We had a provisional budget of €500,000, which was based on the assumption that we would get a good price for the sale of our house in Brussels. If we did, we would be mortgage free, which was really an important part of the move for us. We didn't want the pressure of loan repayments, especially when there was some uncertainty about our future income. To go for the Cadouin property we would have needed some borrowings, which we had agreed we would only consider if we found somewhere that was really fantastic and had great income potential, and this wasn't it.

Tanya was still keen on it but, after a long and sometimes emotional discussion, she agreed that it wasn't the right place for us. With this painful admission, however, came tears – lots of tears – which I think were due to a combination of exhaustion, disappointment and the growing realisation that maybe we were never going to find the right place.

## Beautiful Quercy

Back in Brussels, we didn't discuss French property for a few weeks, even though, secretly, I was still checking websites from time to time. Instead, our attention turned to the summer holidays, and yes, you've guessed it, what part of France we would visit. We might have gone down a blind alley on the property search, but France was still our preferred holiday destination.

We eventually settled on the Lot. During our Easter visit to the Dordogne, which is just north of the Lot, Caroline took us into this neighbouring department to visit two different properties and we really liked the look of it. It seemed just as nice as the Dordogne, with lots of forest and some really pretty villages, but less touristy. Caroline also told us that it was drier and the climate had more of a Mediterranean influence than the Dordogne.

Coincidentally, a few days after we made this decision, a chance conversation with a Belgian acquaintance also led to an interesting and maybe prophetic endorsement. Jean-Paul was in his late fifties – old enough to have sense in other words – and he had been holidaying in France all of his life. So when I got into a conversation with him at a reception one evening, it seemed like a good opportunity to pick his brain. I asked him what his favourite region was. He looked at me with a knowing smile. He didn't even have to think about it.

'Beautiful Quercy', he said, as he stared into the distance.

Quercy? I knew that place. I remembered learning about it at school. I couldn't remember the exact details but I knew that my French teacher had told us about the area and it had left a strong impression on me. The image I had in my mind was of an area lost in time: unspoiled, with pristine river valleys, extensive areas of oak and chestnut forest, and a way of life that had remained largely unchanged for centuries.

I'm not sure I ever really knew where it was, however, what part of France it was, so when Jean-Paul mentioned it, it suddenly came home to me that this was actually a real place, and not some imaginary utopia. I had to know more.

Jean-Paul spoke glowingly about the fantastic nature, the wonderful climate, the great food, the wine, the truffles, the beautiful villages, the people, the rural way of life, the sky, the rivers, the atmosphere, the Zen …. Okay, he had quite a few drinks taken at this stage, but his love of the area was genuine. Jean-Paul described it as being south of the Massif Central, but not as far south as the Mediterranean. I asked him was it near the Dordogne and, as if destiny had somehow preordained it, he said it was just south of there. I wanted to hug him. Quercy, I had just discovered, was in fact the old name for the department of the Lot. I was starting to have a really good feeling about this area.

We booked our holidays: two weeks at the beginning of July, in a gîte near the village of Montcabrier, in the western part of the Lot. My parents were also going to join us for the second week. A few days after we made the booking, towards the end of May, I casually brought up the subject of property again, sensing, wrongly, that Tanya had moved on from the Cadouin experience. She looked at me in disbelief and I could see her eyes welling up. It was too soon. A few weeks later, I tried again, with more success this time, helped by the fact that I had placed some glossy magazines with photos of beautiful French farmhouses and châteaux at various strategic locations throughout the house. After some discussion, she eventually agreed to the idea of organising another viewing, on the condition that we would limit it to one day and that we wouldn't let it ruin our holiday. We also agreed that it would have to be during the first week, as we didn't want to abandon my parents to go property hunting.

In the weeks leading up to the holiday we intensified the online search. We both made long lists of properties we liked in the area, which we then amalgamated into a single long list. And then, mindful of the fact that we would only have one day, we got brutal, and then even more brutal, until we finally ended up with a shortlist of five properties. There were a few last-minute changes to the list as Emily, our new agent, tried to organise the viewings, but it stayed at five.

# 2

# A Coup de Coeur

The day of the holidays finally arrived and boy did we need a holiday. Work had been manic for me, and the strain of two children under three was also taking its toll on us both. With the car weighed to the ground with buggies, suitcases, toys, jumbo-sized packs of nappies, nappy bags, children's potties, and spare jumbo-sized packs of nappies, we hit the road. Nappies and potties really were the story of the day in fact, as we were in the middle of potty-training Ned, so, as you can imagine, it was a trip that did not go without incident. One, in particular, stands out.

Long-distance driving is, of course, completely unsuitable for babies and toddlers. They're forced to sit still for hours, being bribed into keeping quiet with different kinds of snacks and inducements; they can't play; they can't run around and burn off energy; and at this age, the only way they can communicate their frustration is by screaming and shouting. Surprisingly, therefore, things went quite smoothly for most of the day. Our master plan had involved stopping every two hours and Ned had duly obliged every time, so the training and the trip were going well, probably too well. As we approached Limoges, our fortunes began to change, however, and a major emergency erupted when Ned uttered the words we had desperately not wanted to hear between stops – 'Want to do caca!'

Initially, we tried to ignore it, to pretend that he hadn't said anything or that he hadn't really meant it. However, this tactic didn't work for long. As his pleas got increasingly desperate, I accelerated in search of somewhere to pull off the motorway, while Tanya tried to reassure him that we were almost there, to hang in there for a few more minutes. With no service station or lay-by in sight, I pressed even harder on the accelerator, which had an undesired effect on Ned and the poor chap got even more anxious. There was a real state of panic in the car now, as we roared along on the inside lane of the motorway in search of that elusive roadside toilet. Eventually, after what seemed like an eternity, I spotted a sign for a Shell station. I urged the car on and as the exit came into view I felt a sense of relief, and unfortunately, I think Ned did too. As I indicated to turn off at the exit, the poor chap lost the battle. 'Caca coming', he announced.

'Park anywhere, quickly, and I'll grab the potty', Tanya gasped. I pulled up by a large hoarding just inside the entrance to the station. Tanya leaped out, grabbed Ned and the potty and put both of them in the only place she could find that would be safe from the traffic: a platform in front of the large hoarding, which we soon discovered was a large sign welcoming motorists to the station. He was safe from getting run over, but he was now also in full view of everyone entering the station. Not that Ned gave a tuppence – in fact, he seemed to enjoy the attention, as he waved at the bemused occupants of the cars that whizzed by on either side of him. It was all a bit academic at this stage anyway, as the 'caca' had mostly been left behind in the car – on Ned's car seat, on the floor underneath, on the car door, and there was quite a bit on Ned himself and on Tanya. We really were 'in the caca'!

As a parent, you get used to these things, though, and it wasn't long before we were back on the road, with everything and everybody cleaned up, and stocked up again with drinks and food from the service station. At around midnight we arrived at the gîte. It was pitch dark, in the middle of woods, and the two kids were fast asleep in the back of the car. We carried them in, put them in their beds, and then collapsed into our own bed, deciding to leave the unpacking until the following morning.

After breakfast the next morning we met the owners, Pete and Sabine. They had met in London, where they had both worked in the financial services sector, and moved to France about six years earlier. The catalyst for the move was their son, Nathan, who was now almost eight. The more they told us, the more parallels we saw with our own situation, but they were a few steps ahead of us. Having left behind his career as a financial analyst, Pete was now on his second novel, and Sabine was running a successful home staging business. They were also running what seemed to be a very successful tourism business, with four large gîtes. As we got to know Pete and Sabine a little better over the course of the holiday, however, we began to discover that everything wasn't as rosy as it first seemed.

One evening Pete let slip that the amount of work involved in maintaining the property was much more than they had expected and more than they (or he, at least) wanted. At the time, I didn't really grasp what he was saying and mostly I just put it down to Pete having a bad day. What did he have to moan about, anyway, when he was living in paradise? It couldn't be that much trouble, I thought. But there was more to come. Later in the holiday, after we came back from our property viewing, we were filling Pete in on what we had seen when he dropped a small bomb that caught us completely by surprise – he and Sabine were selling up! In fact, they had put their place on the market a couple of years earlier and Pete was now quite irate, firstly about the fact that they had put the place up for sale at the height of the property boom in 2007 and didn't manage to sell it, and secondly, because people were now calling up and offering him half of the original asking price. He was visibly disgusted with these 'bottom fishers', who he accused of trying to exploit the downturn in the market in order to get a bargain. I understood his frustration but, as a former financial analyst in the City of London, I was a bit surprised by his naivety.

From where I was sitting, as a potential buyer, this didn't seem quite as despicable as Pete was portraying it. Was it not just market forces, the same forces that had helped many sellers to bag huge windfalls in the years preceding the downturn? We later discovered that Pete and Sabine were asking a cool €895,000, which was well over our budget, and probably why the estate agent hadn't mentioned it.

On the positive side, they had nothing but good things to say about Emily, who also happened to be their estate agent. We met her for our one day of property viewing on the Wednesday of the first week of our holidays. We liked her; she seemed more open and honest than the other estate agents we had met. As previously agreed, Emily showed us five places that day. Disappointingly, but not surprisingly, none of them lived up to our expectations. By far the best of the five was an old hunting lodge, which was only a couple of kilometres from Pete and Sabine's place, but it needed a lot of work and it was just too expensive.

My parents arrived that weekend and, over a comforting bottle of local Cahors wine, we filled them in on our day's property viewing. Interestingly, they seemed genuinely disappointed that we hadn't found somewhere we liked. I say 'interestingly' because I wasn't sure how my parents felt about our proposed move to France, so it was really nice to discover that they were supportive. I'm sure that they would have preferred us to move back to Ireland and to have their grandchildren nearby but, true to form, they didn't let this get in the way of their desire to see us happy and our plans come to fruition. In fact, at the end of the discussion, they insisted that we go back to the estate agent to see if she had anything else we could look at, while they looked after the kids. We were initially against this idea, as that wasn't why we had invited them to join us on holidays, but my mother can be very persuasive. We also knew that it would be our last opportunity for a year, maybe two, to look at property, so we graciously accepted their offer.

The next morning, in Prayssac, we passed by the estate agents' office. Although it was Sunday and the office was officially closed, Emily's boss, Jill, was inside and she invited us in. Jill pulled out four large folders, which contained all the properties they had on their books. She began to flick through each folder, removing the properties that she thought might be of interest. Half an hour later she had selected about fifteen properties. We went through them one by one and despite our best efforts we just couldn't find that *coup de coeur*. Jill was a determined woman, however, so she started to go through the files again. At this stage, I wasn't holding out much hope, and my mind and eyes started to wander. There were some lovely enlarged photos of properties on the walls of the office, which grabbed my attention. It seemed to be a selection of their best properties, lots of lovely châteaux and large farmhouses, all in that warm, honey-coloured stone that is typical of the Lot.

Unfortunately, they were all well out of our price range, but nice to look at all the same. Then I noticed one that looked familiar. It resembled one of the properties we had seen in the folders and, even though it was over budget, it was within reach. When we had come across it in the folder, Jill had ruled it out immediately, as she said it didn't really fit our criteria and was too expensive. The photo in the catalogue wasn't very appealing so we didn't object, but seeing the larger photo on the wall, my interest was rekindled. I checked with Jill that it was in fact the same property, and she confirmed it was, but again, she discounted it on the basis that it was over our budget and not what we were looking for. I was still curious, so I asked her if we could have another look. She gave me a hard look and, reluctantly, flicked back through the file. When she eventually found the right page she read the details to herself again before declaring that it wasn't suitable for us. I asked her if we could have a look at it, and she gave me another long, hard look. I was really getting on her nerves now, but I held her gaze and said nothing. I was surprised by her attitude; she was making me feel uncomfortable and I didn't know why. She handed me the file, while continuing to insist it wasn't right for us: the internal layout wasn't suitable, it was near the road, and at €630,000 we couldn't afford it, and she didn't believe the owner would drop the price.

She then re-presented her original shortlist of fifteen, which she insisted were the kinds of properties we would get for our budget. Logically, she was right. These were the types of properties that were in our price range, but unfortunately we didn't like any of them. The property that was in the photo on the wall was the one that excited me. It was over budget, but it was the kind of property that we had imagined when we discussed moving to France in the first place. I asked Jill to add this to a shortlist of five properties that we had already agreed on.

'It's pointless', she said. 'I can tell you now that the owner isn't going to drop the price.'

I told her that if we really liked it we might be able to raise our budget a little, but no, she was adamant that this was not the kind of property we were looking for and raising our budget 'a little' would not be enough. The strength of her resistance took us by surprise. I thought that she would at least indulge us on this simple request but she really did not want to concede. Not knowing what else to do, I resorted to pleading with her to show it to us anyway, accepting that she was probably right. At least we could then rule it out for ourselves. Finally, she agreed, but only because she had run out of excuses and she knew I wasn't going to let it go.

§

The following Thursday morning all six of us set off for another day's property viewing. My parents and the children came with us, as we didn't want to leave them at the gîte all day. It was their holiday too, and we had a sneaking suspicion that they were curious about the whole thing. The viewings on this occasion were slightly better than before but there was still nothing to make our hearts flutter. At 5 p.m., we took stock with Emily outside property number five, which was one of the low points of the day: a lovingly restored, but pint-sized cottage, in which the upstairs had been divided up into a ridiculous number of miniature bed-rooms, and for which the English owners were asking the outlandish sum of €550,000. Even Emily admitted that this was nonsensical, but apparently they were not willing to sell for a cent less. Emily then broke the news that we had been half-expecting all day: 'You've really seen the best of what's available now. Are there any of these properties you're inter-ested in, or want to have a second look at?'

The sense of disappointment was palpable. It wasn't like this in the dream. Instead of the perfect house falling into our lap, we were searching for a needle in a haystack. But what about property number six?

'Well, it's getting late, and it's quite a distance away. We can go if you really want but I'm not sure it's worth your while.'

'Yes, we want to, we really want to', I insisted, if for no other reason than to confront what seemed to be some kind of conspiracy to keep us away.

## Domaine de Laborie

It was a beautiful evening; the intense heat of the day had softened and the warm air was laden with the sweet aroma of wild flowers and herbs. Inside the car, the mood was sombre. This was possibly the last property we would look at in France for a long time. It had been a long journey; we had given it our best shot but now we had enough. Strangely, with this realisation came a certain sense of relief. Like a job or sport or other challenges in life, sometimes things just don't work out no matter how hard you try, and there is a real sense of relief when you finally acknowledge this and stop putting pressure on yourself.

The road was a winding, narrow country road, one we hadn't been on before, and in our calmer, more philosophical state of mind, we really began to appreciate the beauty of the countryside, with its sprinkling of small, honey-coloured villages and hamlets, scattered across a patchwork of forests and open pastures. I was really glad we had discovered this part of France, despite the fact that we hadn't yet managed to find a suitable home there. Along the route, we kept ourselves busy trying to guess which property Emily was going to stop at. Every so often a beautiful farmhouse or manor would come into view but, to our disgust, Emily just kept on driving. As we exited yet another of the perfectly preserved medieval hamlets, we noticed another stunning looking property, an impressive Quercy-style château, with the hallmark tower or dovecote, all constructed in big, solid blocks of honey-coloured stone. As we drove by, all twelve eyes peered over the boundary wall, admiring the nobleness of this fine property, adorned by mature orchards and gardens on one side and a row of old stone outbuildings on the other. As we continued on past the gate, an inconsiderate laurel hedge blocked our view, so we settled back into our seats to await what other surprises lay ahead.

About 100 metres or so further on, Emily began to slow down and then indicated and turned left off the road. We followed her through a gated entrance and along a tree-lined avenue, which turned back in the direction we had just come from.

'It can't be', I said, and just then we got a first glimpse of a house at the end of the lane. To our astonishment, it was the same house we had just passed, but this time we had a front view, and we could just about make out two towers, which I immediately recognised from the pictures we had seen in the estate agents' office.

As we continued along the lane, the car started to come to life, and someone excitedly pointed out a swimming pool behind some trees and shrubs to the right, where there were children playing and splashing. At the end of the drive, we could see three women sitting on the grass, just in front of the stone steps that led up onto a covered terrace at the front the house. The scene was quintessentially French. A family scene: parents, children and grandparents all gathered together in the warmth of the evening. It was timeless, and as the house finally came fully into view the picture was complete. It was older-looking than it seemed in the photo and had much more charm.

This was the kind of the property we had been searching for. I was smitten, and Tanya just looked on in a state of disbelief. We were now back in the game, completely and utterly. Despite everything we had seen, this was proof that what we were looking for did actually exist. It might have been a bit more expensive than we expected, but it existed and it was within reach.

Following Emily's lead, we pulled off the lane, parked in between some tress, and walked the remaining 20 metres or so to the house. The place was a hive of activity: teenagers and younger children scurrying back and forth between the house and pool; two separate groups of adults sitting on the grass, deep in conversation; a young woman calling to the children from an upstairs window of the house; and, in the middle of all this commotion, was the serene and mature presence of an older woman, who was now moving towards us.

'Welcome to Domaine de Laborie', she said, extending her hand.

Emily introduced her as the owner of the property, Mrs Sumner, an attractive, well-groomed woman in her late sixties or early seventies. She had a kind, intelligent face and a natural elegance and charisma. I liked her. She made us feel welcome and invited Emily to give us an access-all-areas tour of the property. We started with the house, making our way up the stone steps to the entrance. The front door was made of oak, framed by solid stone pillars. There were no ornate features and few decorative aspects – the beauty was in the materials themselves and the solidness of the construction. It was built to last. The story was the same elsewhere in the house. The best-quality natural materials and craftsmanship were evident everywhere, but it was about functionality and durability rather than frivolity. It was noble, but not ostentatious. The entrance hall was small, considerably smaller than I would have expected, but this thought didn't linger long as our eyes were immediately drawn through an open door into the left, to a very large stone fireplace. This was the kitchen, and it was typically French farm house. Besides the fireplace, there was a lovely old oak table in the centre of the room and an incredible stone sink in the corner, beside the window. The appliances were a bit dated but that didn't matter; it had character.

We continued to make our way through the house room by room and we mostly liked what we saw. At the end of the tour, we ended up in the large living room, where a middle-aged man with long hair and a long, dark beard sat watching television with two young children. As we entered the room, my father looked at me inquisitively and enquired in a low voice:

'What's Saint Patrick doing here?'

'It must be a sign', I ventured.

It was difficult to remember much detail from this first visit, partly because there were people in nearly every room and we didn't want to intrude too much, but also because there was a lot to take in, and we were rushing – it was late and the children were tired. My overall impression, however, was that this was it – the dream home – or at least as close as we were ever likely to get to it. I loved it; it was full

of French rural charm, and it had a nice family feel, accentu-
ated no doubt by the scores of family photos and paintings
on the walls. It had the feel of a house that needed people,
lots of people. At first I wasn't sure that Tanya felt the same
way. She had remained quiet for much of the tour, but as we
turned to leave the living room she turned to me and said
everything I needed to hear: 'I could see us living here.'

We left Saint Patrick and his followers and headed back
outside to explore the grounds – or a small part of the
grounds rather, as there was also a sizable plot of land. On
the way out, Tanya and I stopped for a few minutes to talk to
Mrs Sumner again, while my father and Ned continued on
around the side of the house. My mother had already gone
back to the car with Astrid – another nappy emergency.

Mrs Sumner told us she and her husband had bought the
house twenty years earlier and that they really loved it, and
the area. You could tell she was sincere, so I didn't really feel
the need to ask her why they were leaving; there must have
been a good reason. She walked with us as we continued
after the others to the garden and, as we turned the corner
of the house, I caught sight of my father and Ned shame-
lessly loading up a large plastic bag with the finest of juicy
plums. I walked on ahead of Tanya and Mrs Sumner, trying
to block her view of the plucky plum plunderers, and hoping
that the duo would move along discretely when they saw
us approaching, but not a bit of it – my father's hearing was
not the best anyway, and Ned was too engrossed in the job
at hand to take any notice, so the industrious pair continued
filling their bag and feasting themselves on their fruity find.

'Aren't they gorgeous, Ned?', I could hear my father
remark.

Ned nodded in agreement, as he busily removed the stone
from a large specimen in his hand. It had been a long time
since lunch. But Mrs Sumner didn't seem to mind, and there
were more than enough plums to go around. I counted ten
trees, each one laden with fruit.

We finished the rather short but exciting tour with a warm feeling. It was such a relief to finally view a property that we really liked, and even though the asking price was well over our budget, it had been on the market for almost two years, and property prices were generally falling or stagnating, so there was a chink of light.

§

The next morning we left the Lot for the long drive to Brussels. With a ten-hour journey ahead of us, there was going to be plenty of time to take stock and by the time we hit the A20 motorway the discussion was already in full swing. Very quickly it became clear that it was basically an open and closed case; we literally rubbished everything we had seen except Laborie.

I loved the property. For me, it was easily the highlight of years of property hunting and I was excited about even having the possibility to bid for it. Every time it was mentioned I felt a warm glow radiate through my body. Tanya was equally bowled over. She had finally seen somewhere that felt like it could be our home, which was exciting but also a little bit daunting perhaps, as suddenly the whole idea of moving to France, which had previously been an idea, a distant prospect, now became a real possibility. My mother too was crazy about the place and had a good feeling about it, which was also significant, as she has some kind of sixth sense that I would never ignore.

This outpouring of love for Laborie was all well and good, however we still had the small issue of the price. They were asking for €630,000, which we could not afford. In the climate that prevailed, it might have been reasonable to go in with an offer of €550,000, with a view to reaching a deal somewhere between €580,000 and €600,000, but even this was still outside our price range. In reality, Jill was right – we couldn't afford it.

But the cat was out of the bag now – we had seen it, we had fallen in love with it and, as far as I was concerned, we had to try something. So I started to do the maths in my head. The best-case scenario was that we would get €600,000 for our house in Brussels, which after paying down the mortgage would leave €470,000. Our savings and investments came to another €60,000, which gave us a total of €530,000. But this would also have to include agents' fees and taxes, which would add another €60,000 to €70,000 (estate agents' fees alone are around 8 per cent in France), and renovations, which I estimated would require at least another €100,000 (or more realistically €200,000, but we all live in denial about these things).

Having done this rough calculation in my head, I came to the conclusion that we would need to get it for around €470,000 to make it any way affordable, and this would mean putting most of the renovations on the long finger, which I was prepared to do, and I guessed Tanya was as well. But this was still too low. At I stretch, I thought we could probably add another €10,000 to our savings before the deal went through, so I arrived at the magic figure of €480,000. This was a long way short of the asking price, but it was really the upper end of what we could afford. With this figure in my head, I decided to test the audience.

'I suppose we could always make an offer; we have nothing to lose', I suggested, waiting patiently for a reaction.

Nothing!

I looked over at Tanya and I could see her eyes watering. This was not the reaction I was looking for; she was clearly interpreting this as a done deal, which was far from being the case. But, then again, she had probably assumed I was talking about a competitive offer, which was also far from being the case.

'What kind of offer?', said Tanya, doing her best to fight back the tears.

'I'm not sure, what do you think?'

I wasn't ready just yet to announce my figure. I feared it would not be well received, especially now that Tanya was already getting her hopes up, so I was waiting for someone else to break the ice.

Nobody said a word.

'We could offer €480,000', I said, boldly. 'If you think about it, it's been on the market a couple of years, they've already dropped the price from €750,000 and they still haven't had any offers, so it's obviously way over-priced', I added quickly, anticipating a mini-riot.

There was silence in the back of the car, except for Astrid, who was performing a drum roll with a marker and an empty water bottle, unknowingly providing a very fitting soundtrack for the tense discussion that was unfolding. Back in the front, Tanya looked horrified.

'They'll never accept that; it's way too low', she snapped, clearly unhappy with my daring plan. The drumming stopped.

'I was thinking more like €580,000 or €590,000 and maybe they would accept something around €600,000. I definitely wouldn't go lower than €550,000', she insisted. She was right, of course. To secure a deal, these were the kinds of figures we needed to be talking about, but the bottom line was that we didn't have that kind of money. On top of that, I still thought the sellers were expecting too much and that at the price Tanya was proposing we would probably be paying over the odds. Property prices were still falling in France and no one really knew where they were going to end. I bombarded Tanya with all the market statistics I could think of, and talked her through our own financial situation in some detail. Eventually, and reluctantly, she agreed to my proposal. My parents were a bit punch drunk by the figures being bandied around but they also agreed it was worth a try.

Back in Brussels the following Monday morning, I phoned Emily with an offer of €480,000. She didn't discount it out of hand, which I was relieved about, but she did have some reservations about putting it to the vendor. It was a big drop and I think she expected a frosty response, but in the end she agreed to give it a go. She said it would probably be the following day before she would have a response but, as it turned out, she called back later that afternoon. The answer was no. It was emphatic; there was no counter proposal, no ifs, no buts, and no maybes. It was 'NO!'

Even though I had been half-expecting this, I was still very disappointed. I had at least hoped for some kind of nego-tiation, but they obviously thought our offer was not even within a range where they could begin to negotiate.

It felt now like the French project was well and truly over. Tanya too was devastated. She was also a bit peeved with me for going in with such a low offer, even though she acknowl-edged that this was the limit of what we could afford. It was hard to accept, for both of us. After almost ten years of dream-ing, planning and searching, that was it. We had found one place that we liked, one property that came anywhere near matching our criteria and budget, and now it had slipped through our fingers. One phone call and it was all over.

§

That was 30 July 2009 and for the next couple of months we settled back into our life in Brussels and never even spoke about property, let alone French property. Even more telling was the fact that I wasn't even tempted into any clandestine web searching. Well, maybe just once or twice, but this was out of habit rather than any real conviction as, at this point in time, we had genuinely given up.

# 3

# A Second Chance

The routine of life in Brussels soon took over again. I was busy at work, Ned started pre-school, and Tanya was occupied with Astrid, who still hadn't celebrated her first birthday. Even if we wanted, we didn't have the time or the energy to resurrect the French project. It started to feel like we were trapped again. We had done everything we could but it hadn't worked out.

Deep down, I knew we would be back property hunting in France again someday, possibly with a bigger budget, but it looked like that was some years off and I was finding it difficult to accept this and knuckle down again. However, life has a way of throwing up surprises, and it was at this point, when we had all but resigned ourselves to at least several more years in Brussels, that we were thrown a lifeline.

On 6 October 2009 we got the call from Emily to say that if we were still interested, the vendors would be willing to reconsider our offer on Laborie. This was a bolt from the blue. Despite all my arguments and reasoning in relation to falling property prices and the buyer's market and the like, I really didn't believe we would ever get a second chance. It was a surprise but a very pleasant one. That evening we celebrated in our local bar. It was still far from a done deal, but there was hope, a reason to be cheerful and optimistic again, and that was enough for now.

Emily had suggested that we go down to the Lot again as soon as possible to have another look at the property. We decided we should act quickly, so we arranged to go down that weekend. To make the best use of the trip, we also made plans to look at another property in the Corrèze, which was on our way.

We set off at 8.30 a.m. on Friday 9 October. Ned had graduated from the school of potty training by then, so it was a less eventful trip, although not completely without incident. We arrived at the property in the Corrèze just after 6 p.m. The agent, Nicolas, was already there, standing by his car, chatting to a woman called Marie-Claire, who he introduced as the owner of the property. Nicolas later explained that she and her husband were going through a divorce, which is why they were selling the house. It appeared they had bought the place about five years earlier and had invested a considerable amount of money, time and emotional energy in the renovation, obviously to the detriment of their marriage. This wasn't the first time we had heard this story during our property search.

It had taken us a while to find the place, but our first impressions were good. It was an old farm complex, with a relatively modest cottage, an enormous barn and two other decent-sized outbuildings, all constructed in the typical style of the area, with local stone, which was a kind of dark grey colour. All the buildings had been recently renovated, except the cottage, the owners' accommodation. Obviously they had focused on getting the income-generating parts of the property completed first, but I couldn't help thinking that it might have been better for their marriage if they had done things the other way round. Looking around the property, it was clear that they had done a lot of work, but with low-cost materials. It wasn't really to our taste and it would need considerable investment to change things to how we would want it. The original asking price had been €714,000 but this had recently been reduced to €475,000. Nicolas told us it was a steal at this price, but I wasn't convinced, and I knew he wasn't either. Given the late hour, we decided to sleep on it and meet him at his office the next morning.

We pulled up outside the office just before 9 a.m. The kids were already in full swing so we decided that Tanya would stay with them in the car while I met Nicolas. We didn't want any distractions and, in any event, I didn't intend staying long. When I entered the office, Nicolas was sitting behind his desk, fiddling with his computer and generally pretending to be busy.

'Good morning Eamon and how are you today?', he said, barely looking up from the computer.

'Very well, thanks, Nicolas, and yourself?'

'Jolly good, jolly good, but I must just finish some urgent matters so please, do take a seat.'

He continued to stare at the computer for a few more minutes and then began ranting about all the problems he was having with the Gîtes de France website, and with swimming pool contractors and a number of other things that I had little interest in. After another five minutes of this I had to stop him. I didn't know exactly what he was up to but it was obvious that he was trying to play some kind of game and I didn't want any part of it.

'Tanya and the kids are waiting outside, Nicolas, so just briefly, about the house, we're still interested but not at anywhere near the current asking price.'

He remained fixated on his computer. It was getting quite annoying now.

'So you like it then, yes?'

'We like it but it would require quite a lot of work to turn it into something that suits our needs.' I proceeded to list off all the negatives from our perspective and for these reasons I explained to him that we wouldn't be prepared to pay any more than about €350,000. I had expected him to fall off the chair at this stage, but he seemed completely unfazed.

'It's quite a bit lower than the owners are expecting but, why not make an offer?' At last he looked me in the eye. 'You must try. As I said before, they're keen to sell. You have to try it.'

Just then the kids came barging through the door. They had been going berserk in the car, so Tanya had been forced to release them, and, having ransacked the car, they now set about doing the same to Nicolas' office. I decided to bring them outside for a while and give Tanya a few minutes with Nicolas. As I was going out the door I could hear him starting off again about the Gîtes de France website and swimming pool contractors. A short while later she came back out and asked me if I had made an offer. She said that Nicolas had told her he would let us know later what the owners thought. I was a bit alarmed by this as I hadn't actually made an offer, and I didn't want it to be interpreted like that, so I went back in to see Nicolas again. He was looking eager, like a man who really wanted to press on and close the deal, so when I asked him to say nothing to the owner until we called him the following Monday, I could sense his unease. I explained to him again that we had arranged a second viewing of a property in the Lot, which we really needed to see before we could make any decisions. I assured him that we would let him know first thing on Monday morning.

'Is it a nice house, the one you're going to look at?', he asked forlornly.

'Yes, it seemed nice enough on the first viewing, but to be honest Nicolas, we would really need to see it again. In any case, we won't decide anything until Monday.'

'You won't forget to call me then?'

'No we won't forget Nicolas, but we really have to go now. Have a nice weekend, and talk to you Monday.'

He didn't reply. He refused to acknowledge that I was leaving. I half expected him to follow me out the door and tackle me to the ground as I desperately tried to make my way to the car.

I started the car quickly and got on the road. On the way out of Argentat I told Tanya the whole story, including his calm response to my suggestion of €350,000.

'You've some balls', she said, looking at me rather fondly.

At that very moment, my mobile phone rang. I was driving so I handed it to Tanya.

'I bet it's him,' I said in jest, 'trying to lure us back to the office again.'

'Hello. Oh Nicolas. Yes, it's Tanya.'

I couldn't believe it. We were less than five minutes into the journey. The tenacity of the guy was unreal. He proceeded to tell Tanya that there was someone else due to visit the property that afternoon, at 2 p.m., some big French company that bought up properties and turned them into holiday centres. He had obviously put his thinking cap on after we left the office, but this was a bit far-fetched, and I found it hard to believe that he would have forgotten to mention something like this when we met earlier. But even if it was true, we had told him already, several times, that we would only make a decision after we saw the property in the Lot.

Tanya thanked him for this 'new information' and told him that we would call him after we had seen the place in the Lot. A few minutes later, as we were still trying to get our heads around his incredible persistence, the phone rang again. Guess who? And this time, he really had gone too far. Tanya answered the phone again and he told her that he knew we asked him not to contact the owner, but he did anyway, and the property could be ours for €320,000. Yes, €320,000, even less than the €350,000 I had indicated we might be willing to pay.

'€320,000!', said Tanya, looking expectantly at me. My eyes widened, but then collapsed under the weight of a heavy frown, as it dawned on me just how cheeky he had been.

'I just need to speak to Eamon first, but I'll call you back in a few minutes.'

There was some more frantic muttering on the other end of the phone.

'Okay Nicolas, you can call me if you prefer, but can you leave it for about ten minutes.'

We just looked at each other in amazement. What was going on here? Were they really that desperate to sell? Were things really that bad in the property market? It all felt a bit strange, but good at the same time. It finally looked like the market was going our way and we might be able to find something we liked, within our budget.

Despite this, we were still keen to see the house in the Lot, and the way things were unfolding in the Corrèze, I was beginning to feel like maybe we were in a stronger position than I had originally thought.

Three minutes later, the phone rang again. Nicolas was clearly in no mind to wait ten minutes. Tanya thanked him for his efforts, despite the fact that we had asked him not to contact the owners, but told him, once again, that we still had to see the place in the Lot. He seemed to take it better this time for some reason. Maybe he was satisfied that he had done just about all he could at this stage, or maybe he was confident that this would be enough to bring us crawling back on our hands and knees the following Monday.

'The ball is in your court', he advised, and we continued on to the Lot.

## Nightmare in Martassac

It was mid-afternoon when we got to the house in the Lot. It was a nice day, sunny and still quite warm for mid-October. We were greeted at the end of the drive by the owner, Mrs Sumner, and the estate agent, Jill. The house looked just as impressive as it did on our first visit. As I walked up the stone steps I just knew that this was the place for us, and everything thereafter only reaffirmed this. I could tell Tanya was on the same wavelength; during the visit I caught several glimpses of a woman trying desperately to contain herself. Oh no, poor Nicolas, I thought to myself.

After Jill showed us around the house, she then proposed that she and Mrs Sumner would sit with the children on the terrace, while Tanya and I took another look by ourselves. This was a real treat I have to say, for which we thanked them profusely. We wandered around the house from room to room, excited and giddy. We didn't say much. We didn't have to; our animated facial expressions said it all. At the top of the stairs we stopped and held each other. At last it seemed like it was all coming together, that there was light at the end of the tunnel, and feelings we had lost sight of for far too long were finally finding some expression again. This was the life we wanted, there was no mistake.

After the visit we sat for a while with Jill and Mrs Sumner on the terrace. Mrs Sumner seemed to like us, and she liked the idea of a family living in the house. We also liked her. She still had those bright intelligent eyes that I remembered from our first visit, but she seemed more serene this time. At first I put this down to her possible sadness at knowing she might be leaving the house in the near future, but later Jill explained that her partner had died not long after our previous visit. This also seemed to be a factor in her decision to try to progress the sale of the house.

It was almost 7 p.m. when we left Laborie that evening, so we agreed to meet Jill at her office the next morning to discuss it further. In the meantime, we made our way to our hotel in Martassac. It was basic, and the rooms were small and a bit dated, but it was close to Laborie and it was the only accommodation we could find in the area. We put the children to bed and then went downstairs to the restaurant. Normally we wouldn't do this, but we seemed to be the only guests in the hotel that weekend and as the kids were quickly asleep we decided to make an exception. We plugged in the baby monitor and headed downstairs. We ate alone in the vast dining room that evening and spoke excitedly about

Laborie, impatiently taking turns listing off our favourite bits and sharing ideas for how we would make the place even more magnificent. In our own minds, we had effectively bought it at this stage. It was now just a question of the price, and the better price we got it for, the more we would have available for the renovations. The main works would involve creating more rentable accommodation. There was already a one-bedroom apartment in the barn and our plan was to convert the rest of the barn, and also to create some B&B accommodation in the main house.

When we arrived at the estate agents' office the next morning, Jill was already inside. She wasn't one for idle chit-chat or speaking off the cuff – she spoke only when she had something to say. I'm not unlike this myself, but Jill made me look like an amateur, and after a couple of minutes of staring at each other in silence I started to feel uncomfortable, so I launched into telling her our position: we did want to make an offer but not the €480,000 we had previously offered. On the basis that property prices were still falling, and were likely to continue to fall for some time, and given the obvious absence of other interested parties, I told her that we now felt that our original offer was too high. I also told her that it now looked like we would have to accept a lower price than expected for our own property in Brussels, which was true, and, of course, I recounted the story of what happened in the Corrèze.

Jill didn't seem too surprised that we had decided to reduce our offer. She did say that she thought our original offer of €480,000 would now be accepted, but she did not know if a lower offer would be. She asked what kind of figure we had in mind, but at this stage I didn't want to say. I didn't want to appear too aggressive or too heartless, especially given the fact that Mrs Sumner had recently lost her partner, so I asked her what she thought would be a reasonable offer. Not surprisingly, she refused to be drawn on this and wouldn't commit a figure. I pressed her to give us some guidance but she gave nothing, which I found frustrating.

After about twenty minutes of fruitless probing, interjected by long silences, my nerves finally gave way. I could hardly believe the words coming out of my mouth: 'I was thinking of a figure of around €350,000', I said in a confident voice, as my legs went weak and my palms began to sweat. I had no idea where this came from, it just came out. Tanya's face fell to the floor, thankfully out of sight of Jill, who appeared to stay calm and collected. There was a short pause, which seemed to last for a fortnight. I had overdone it, I knew I had, but I couldn't retract it now, I would look even more stupid. I had to sit tight and let Jill respond. What was she waiting for? I needed her to say something, preferably that it was a respectable first bid and we could discuss it.

At last, her lips moved … no, false alarm. She remained speechless and expressionless. Obviously this was not what she wanted to hear, and certainly not what she wanted to tell her client. Her head turned, she sighed and gave me a passing glance, but still the same expressionless look. I had no idea what she was thinking. It was freaking me out. Maybe she thought I was just a silly git. Finally, she spoke: 'I really don't think that would be accepted.'

It was brief and to the point but she didn't completely rubbish it, which would not have been her style anyway. The shock therapy did seem to have an effect, however, and at last she began to talk more freely. She said that she felt the 'psychological limit' was €400,000, but that in her opinion we would need to be closer to €480,000. Tanya called me aside and whispered €450,000 into my ear, but with the memory of the Corrèze still fresh in my mind I was convinced we could get a better deal. The fact that Jill had already identified a psychological limit also gave me a more definite marker.

'Okay, well let's go with an offer of €400,000 then', I suggested.

I knew this was still the very lower end of what would be an acceptable offer, but I felt it was worth a try and it gave us room for negotiation. Jill remained expressionless, simply accepting our instruction and agreeing to put the offer to Mrs Sumner.

As we had already arranged to have lunch in the café next door, she said she would come and find us there to let us know the answer. We ate lunch in the café, checking the door for Jill every two minutes. We had starters, then main course, but there was still no sign of Jill. Having finished dessert and coffee, including several refills, we were starting to get anxious. In fact, I wasn't feeling well at all; I think the combination of anxiety and several cups of strong coffee had left me feel a bit nauseous, so I decided to take a walk outside to get some air and also to see if Jill was still in her office. I strolled up the street past the office but, annoyingly, with the glare of the sun on the window, I couldn't see inside.

I went back to the café and drank more coffee, which really gave me the heebie-jeebies. I didn't feel well and I desperately needed to lie down, but as this wasn't possible, I decided to take another walk outside. This time, I was just outside the door when I spotted Jill walking towards me. She told me she hadn't been able to reach Mrs Sumner, but would try again in the afternoon and let us know. She played down our chances, and seemed a bit colder than she had been a couple of hours earlier. But despite this, she persisted with the maxim she had used earlier, 'nothing ventured, nothing gained', which I interpreted as a sign that she didn't disapprove of our offer. She promised to call as soon as she had any news.

I went back inside the café and told Tanya, who, like me, smelt a fish. We found it hard to believe that Mrs Sumner was non-contactable, especially as she knew we were meeting that morning and that we were pretty likely to make an offer. I was also struck by the change in Jill's demeanour, and it had been over two hours since we left her office, so I was pretty sure she had spoken to someone, or maybe even to several people. What they might have been talking about, I had no idea, but perhaps they were discussing some kind of counter-strategy. Maybe she had called her husband, Edward, who was also involved in the business, and they were trying to mobilise one of their friends or family members to make a better offer and cut us out of the picture. This might also explain why they were so reluctant to show us the property in the first place. The strong coffee was making me paranoid.

As the afternoon wore on, we grew increasingly agitated, continuously checking our phones for missed calls or messages, but there was nothing. In the vacuum in which we now found ourselves, our minds started to play tricks on us and we began to imagine all kinds of weird conspiracies – Jill, Edward, Mrs Sumner, they were all characters in some twisted plot to prevent us from getting the house. By evening we were in a bit of a state, and quite annoyed that Jill had not even bothered to call us back to let us know what was happening. We must have called her mobile phone at least ten times during the day, and left several voice messages, but still she had not responded.

We were back at the hotel at this stage, having spent most of the afternoon driving around, supposedly getting to know the area, but really just trying to keep our minds occupied. Now, in the rather gloomy surroundings of our small, two-star hotel room, there was no escape. I felt exhausted and trapped, both physically and mentally, and I slowly started to descend into some kind of strange, psychotic state that would persist for the rest of the weekend. There were so many thoughts going through my head that I didn't know whether I was coming or going. Partly, I was feeling guilty that I might have been taking advantage of a woman who had just lost her husband and was desperate to sell up and move on. At the same time, however, I also felt an obligation to my own young family. We couldn't go back to looking at more properties, we had pushed that to the limit, but it seemed like our happiness depended on the move. This had to work out and we had to get it at the right price. Tanya seemed to be less caught up in the emotion of it all. She was slightly annoyed that I hadn't made a higher offer but, at the same time, she didn't see why Mrs Sumner's personal situation should be an issue – we were simply making an offer, which she was under no obligation to accept if she didn't like it. She was probably right, but I still felt uncomfortable.

I didn't sleep much that night and I was glad to see the sun finally come up the next morning. It was Sunday, and I was hopeful that we would be able to speak to Jill during the course of the morning. We checked my phone again, and Tanya's, but still nothing. After breakfast, I decided to call Jill on her mobile again but, as before, it went straight to voicemail.

We spent a good part of the day driving up and down past the house, peering longingly over the wall, and planning various improvements and renovations as we waited, anxiously, for news from Jill. Frustratingly, the whole day went by and still nothing. We checked our phones almost every ten minutes, but there was not even a text message. By evening we were completely exhausted from the waiting and wondering. Why had Jill not phoned to let us know what was happening? When I left her on Saturday, she had promised to phone that afternoon. Did she really not understand how anxious we were to hear from her?

By 9 p.m., we finally resigned ourselves to the fact that, once again, there would be no news that day. We were back seated in the corner of the football-pitch-sized restaurant at the hotel, the only guests again that night, and our imaginations were running wild. Had Jill been so disgusted with our offer that she decided not to contact Mrs Sumner? Maybe, but she seemed happy enough to go through with it when we discussed it in her office, even though her attitude seemed to have changed when I met her on the street afterwards. Maybe she called her colleagues and they advised her not to go any further with it. Or, maybe she was just letting us sweat it out, hoping that we would crack and come back with a better offer. Maybe – and maybe our offer was genuinely too low, which was also something that had crossed my mind.

I didn't sleep very well again that night, and when I finally did nod off, the nightmares I had were even worse than my waking thoughts. I woke at 1.30 a.m. in a cold sweat and shook Tanya until she was half awake. I had to tell her about my new plan – we would have to raise our offer – poor Mrs Sumner has had a difficult time, it was not fair to be too hard on her. Tanya mumbled something that sounded like 'cabbage patch' and then turned and went back to sleep. I lay awake for another hour, analysing my new plan. My heart was now very firmly in control of my head. I was exhausted and Mrs Sumner's situation was really troubling me; I desperately wanted some kind of resolution. I reached down beside the bed for my holdall. I knew I had packed a calculator somewhere and I wanted to go over the figures again. I tapped away for about an hour, trying various options and scenarios and in the end I came up with a magic figure of €420,000. We would have to call Jill to tell her we wanted to raise our offer. But it was only 3.30 a.m.; I would have to wait a few hours.

# 4

## Happy Monday

I had just managed to get back to sleep, having finalised the master plan, when I was awoken again by the sound of Ned calling me next door. It was 4.05 a.m. I fumbled in the direction of the children's room to see what was wrong. He was wide awake and wanted to get up. I tried to settle him but it was no use. At 4.30 he was still protesting and it really didn't look like he was going to go back to sleep, so I went back to Tanya and persuaded her that we should just leave the hotel and get on the road; I thought that we might as well get the journey under way as lying in bed, hopelessly trying to get to sleep. She wasn't too pleased, but she agreed, so we packed our things, and then I went back to pick up Ned. I pushed back the door and there he was, fast asleep, the picture of innocence. Astrid too – both of them were in a deep sleep. This is so typical of kids, they can turn it on and off at the drop of a hat, but there was no turning back now; we had to try to get them into the car.

Tanya set off first with Astrid, but as soon as she woke and realised what was happening her screeching almost brought the roof down. I stayed behind trying, awkwardly, to load Ned onto my back without waking him. I eventually settled for getting him into my arms, and then I got the crazy idea of also trying to drag along one of our massive suitcases. I was able to wheel the suitcase as far as the stairs, but then I realised I would have to lift it, along with Ned. Momentarily, I thought about leaving it at the top of the stairs and coming back for it later, but I really just wanted to get loaded up and on the road as soon as possible, so, like a heavyweight lifter, I went down, knees bent, and lifted the 25-kilo suitcase. Halfway down the stairs I started to wobble, and I felt something strange going on in my lower back and around my hips. By the time I got to the bottom of the stairs it felt like I was at least 2 inches shorter and I had the gait of a 110-year-old woman. I limped past Tanya, who was on her way back in, too wound up to even speak.

We finally got on the road at 5 a.m. My back was aching, I was tired and hungry, the children were whinging, Tanya wasn't speaking to me, and we still had not heard from Jill. To make matters worse, it was lashing rain and still dark, so the gloomy feeling inside the car also extended well beyond its limits. I must have done some terrible things in my past life to deserve this, I thought to myself. Not long into the journey, Ned and Astrid nodded off to sleep again and, as it approached dawn, the rain slowly began to fizzle out. After we stopped for coffee and croissants the mood swing was complete – even the pain in my back began to ease up. With the children asleep and the mood softening, Tanya and I had a few quiet moments to make up and to take stock of the trip. It hadn't turned out as we expected. It got off to a promising start in the Corrèze, but it had been downhill from there. Jill was the main focus of our disappointment. What kind of game was she playing with us?

At 9 a.m. we tried to call her again, but the same familiar voicemail message kicked in. This must have been the tenth message we left, on top of thirty or forty missed calls, so if there was a genuine reason for her silence, which was possible, she was going to think we were total crackpots. As the morning wore on we tried to call Jill several more times, but still no response. We also tried Emily and the office number, but to no avail. Eventually, at around 11.30 a.m., we finally got a response, but it wasn't Jill or Emily – it was Tom.

We had never heard of Tom before, but he said he was the new office assistant. Tanya asked to speak to Jill, explaining that we had been trying to contact her all weekend and all morning, but according to Tom neither Jill nor Emily was in the office. He said he would try to contact them and ask one of them to call us back immediately. A short while later, he phoned back to tell us that Jill was with some clients and was in an area where she did not have a good signal on her mobile phone, but she would try to call us that evening. He had not been able to reach Emily. We thought it was a bit strange that Tom was able to get in touch with Jill so quickly, given that we had been trying all morning, and especially as she was supposedly in an area with a bad signal.

The idea of waiting another full day for news from Jill didn't sit well with Tanya and she made this known to Tom, who then promised to keep trying to reach Emily. Another thirty minutes passed and still there was no news from Tom or Emily. The mood was tense in the car now. It was starting to look like yet another day without any news from Jill. In one last-ditch attempt to find out what was going on, I decided to phone the office and yell down the phone at whoever answered to see if that would have any effect. We pulled off the motorway at the next service station and I got out of the car with the phone, not wanting the children to hear my raised voice. Tom answered and he promised me that Emily would call me back within ten minutes. How he could suddenly be so certain of this I don't know but, true to his word, about eight minutes later Emily called me back. We told her the story and she acted, pretty convincingly, as if she wasn't aware of any of it. She may have been telling the truth, but at this stage I really didn't trust anyone at the estate agency. She said she would try to speak to Jill or Mrs Sumner and get back to us with some news as soon as possible.

While waiting for Emily to call back we decided to get some lunch in the service station restaurant. It was quiet in the restaurant, so we served ourselves quickly at the buffet counter and had just sat down at a table when the phone rang again. It was Emily. I was expecting her to tell me that she still hadn't been able to contact Jill or Mrs Sumner, but I was pleasantly surprised: 'Hi Eamon. Now, I've managed to speak to Jill and she says that Mrs Sumner would not accept the offer of €400,000. ... However, she would accept €420,000.'

I looked at Tanya, somehow managing to keep a straight face.

'Okay. And does that include agents' fees?'

Tanya lifted her head and looked at me.

'Yes, I think so. I'll have to confirm that but I'm almost certain it does.'

'Can you hold for a second Emily? I just want to have a quick word with Tanya.'

I knew Tanya would agree, but I didn't want it to seem like we were willing to raise our offer without a discussion. I held my hand over the phone and whispered to Tanya.

'She won't accept €400,000, but she will go for €420,000. What do you think?'

Tanya was in shock, but she nodded excitedly in affirmation, as I knew she would.

'Emily, we're happy to go with that.'

'Okay, great, I'll call Mrs Sumner now and get back to you shortly.'

Ten minutes later, Emily phoned back and confirmed that Mrs Sumner had accepted the €420,000 offer, including agents' fees.

I cannot describe what a relief it was and how ecstatic we felt on hearing this news. After the intensity of the previous two days and the disappointment of years of searching without finding what we were looking for, it was hard to believe that we had finally done it – it was real; we were moving to France.

There were emotional scenes in the service station restaurant that day – we hugged and kissed and then all four of us joined in a group hug around Astrid's baby chair. To bystanders it probably looked like we had just won the lottery – and to us, it felt like we had. We were on a high the whole way home, and, despite the exhaustion, we still had the energy to plan the house warming in great detail. We completed the entire guest list, decided on the sleeping arrangements and even agreed on the menu.

# 5

## Blue Tuesday

Things moved quickly when we got back to Brussels. The following Tuesday we sent copies of our passports and other details, and on Wednesday the *compromis de vente* (preliminary but binding contract) arrived by e-mail. There were a few minor surprises – firstly, Mrs Sumner wanted to close the sale before the end of the year, for tax reasons (she would save €15,000), as it turned out that the property was not actually owned by Mrs Sumner, but by an offshore company, a trust, of which she was the sole beneficiary. Mrs Sumner also wanted to stay on in the house until the end of February 2010.

We agreed to both of these requests, and from our side there was only one condition – a survey of the building. Emily had agreed to organise this and to give us a verbal report from the property, so that we could then go ahead and sign the contract as quickly as possible. She was on-site the next morning with an architect acquaintance and after the survey she called to tell us that everything was fine. A few hours later she called back again, but this time the news was less positive: just as she was about to leave the property after the survey, things took an unexpected twist – two people arrived to view the house. Emily was horrified and asked Mrs Sumner what was going on, but she insisted that it was just a precaution, in case the sale fell though (which had happened on two previous occasions). Emily assured us that she had made it clear to Mrs Sumner that this wasn't acceptable, but she said that Mrs Sumner confirmed that she fully intended to honour her agreement with us. The only thing we could do now was to sign the contract and get it back to Emily as quickly as possible.

We read it again, signed it and sent it by registered post the following morning. We had hoped it would be with the *notaire* (solicitor) and signed by the vendor before the week-end – we didn't trust weekends when it came to this property – but unfortunately the Belgian and/or French postal system let us down and it only arrived the following Monday morning. We then discovered that the directors of the trust, who were based in London and Guernsey, had to assign power of attorney to the *notaire* in France before the signing could be completed. However, the trust's solicitor in London had been away and would only receive the documents the following morning. They would then have to be sent to Guernsey and then back to London, before finally being dispatched to France. This could take weeks.

'Yes, possibly two to three weeks', Emily conceded.

This was not good, especially as we knew that the house was still being viewed, and until the contracts were signed by the vendors the sale had no legal basis. I had an uncomfortable feeling in my gut. By the following weekend we were still in a state of limbo, with nothing signed. The high of the initial acceptance of our offer had now subsided and we were back to a more familiar state, one of anxiety: hypothesising about what might happen, the ifs, buts and maybes – even Jill went back under the microscope, as we still hadn't figured out why she had not contacted us.

Weekends were really the enemy in this situation, as nobody was contactable and nothing was getting done, so I was glad when Monday morning arrived, even though there was still no further news. On Tuesday, I was busy at work when I had a call from Tanya. We had a viewing of our own house that morning so when she whispered in a low voice, 'There's been an offer of €90,000 more', my overloaded brain initially made the wrong link.

There was silence for a couple of seconds – Tanya was allowing time for me to absorb the news, and I was trying to figure out what this meant and why she was being so quiet and downbeat; it didn't seem to make sense. Then the penny dropped, and I could feel my heart sinking into my shoes.

Tanya started to sob and as she did my initial shock turned to anger. How could Mrs Sumner do this? She had accepted our offer in good faith, and after Emily discovered she was still allowing viewings, she gave her word again that she would respect our agreement. I was furious and, rather than console Tanya, who was now crying on the other end of the phone, I immediately set about trying to devise a plan. But first I needed to know exactly what happened and I tried, impatiently, to extract this from my poor distressed wife.

The story, as she heard it from Jill, was that a couple who had viewed the house after our offer was accepted had made an offer of €510,000. At first I thought that maybe this was just a ploy to get us to raise our offer, but Jill had assured Tanya that the offer was genuine. I don't know how she knew this, but she was adamant – it wasn't a ploy. We needed time to think, but in the meantime Tanya called Emily. After all, Mrs Sumner had promised Emily that she wouldn't accept other offers and I had confidence in Emily that she wouldn't let her away with this. An hour later, Tanya phoned me back. There was another twist to the story: a third offer had been made, this time for €520,000, and, even worse, it was a cash buyer, who was dealing directly with Mrs Sumner, so there were no agents' fees to factor in. According to Jill it was a local Dutch couple. And there was more bad news: Emily was on a week's holiday.

We found it hard to believe the news of the third offer. Why, after the property had been on the market for three or four years, with no serious offers, would two buyers just come out of the woodwork like this in the space of a few hours (and, conveniently, in the week when Emily just happened to be on holidays)? Jill insisted again that the offers were genuine, so we had to take it seriously.

At this stage I still thought there was hope. We had an agreement – okay it was only verbal, but in my moral code-book an agreement is an agreement and I was still confident that it had to stand for something. I phoned Jill later that afternoon and tried to impress this on her. She listened but insisted that our verbal agreement had no legal standing. She also asked me what I would do if I was in Mrs Sumner's situation and I had verbally accepted an offer and then someone offered me an extra €100,000. I wanted to give her an honest answer, so I took a moment to think about it.

'If I had accepted an offer and given my word on it, as Mrs Sumner has done, I would honour it. It would be painful, but I would do it. I might try to appeal to the person who had made the original offer to raise their bid, but at the end of the day I would honour the original agreement', I replied.

My high moral standards took me a bit by surprise, and Jill too I think, but I really did mean what I said, and I couldn't think of any previous event in my life that would have contradicted it. Okay, our original offer to Mrs Sumner may have been low and opportunistic, but it was honest and transparent and she had the option of rejecting it.

I asked Jill to go back to Mrs Sumner one more time to express our devastation at this news and to let her know that we still expected her to honour our agreement. I wasn't convinced that Jill was the best person to do this. I would have much preferred that it was Emily, but we had no choice, and if everything we were being told was true then it was in Jill's interest not to lose the sale either.

Jill called me back about an hour later to report on her discussion with Mrs Sumner. It seems she did feel some moral obligation towards us, but this was being outweighed by the prospect of the extra money, some considerable pressure from another family member, and, apparently, a slight feeling of disappointment about our low offer. The upshot of this was that Jill was now convinced that Mrs Sumner was going to accept the higher offer, unless of course we could match it or go very close. By very close, her best guess was that we would have to go back to our original offer of €480,000, plus agent's and *notaire*'s fees, which would bring the cost to over €550,000.

The situation looked bleak, but I still wasn't ready to throw in the towel. I felt sure that if I could just speak to Mrs Sumner directly I could convince her to stick with us, that we could find some kind of a compromise. I asked Jill if she would talk to Mrs Sumner and see if she would agree to take a call from me directly. Jill didn't hold out much hope, but a short while later she called back to say that Mrs Sumner was surprised by my request, but she agreed.

## End Game

I sat alone in my small office in the upstairs of our house in Brussels. It was late evening and already dark outside. I picked up the receiver and dialled Mrs Sumner's number. The phone rang; I could feel my heart beat. It rang once more and then Mrs Sumner answered. I introduced myself and asked if she was free to speak. She said she was with someone and asked if I could call her back in fifteen minutes. I agreed, hung up and waited in my office, watching the minutes slip by and slowly getting more and more anxious – this had to work. Tanya was downstairs with the kids and her brother and his son, who were visiting us at the time. I knew if I went back down and told her it was gone she would be devastated. There was no other way, it just had to work.

Exactly fifteen minutes later, I called back. Mrs Sumner answered again. I thanked her for taking the call and then I made my pitch – I explained how we were very surprised and disappointed about what had happened, especially as we had trusted and believed her when she reassured Emily that she would not accept any other offers. She apologised, but explained that she had a family of seven, plus grandchildren, so she couldn't ignore the higher offer. She also asked if we could not still go for the other house we had visited in the Corrèze (Jill must have told her about that). There was no doubt that she had made up her mind to go with the higher cash offer and it was clear to me at this stage that the reason she had agreed to take my call was to get me to accept this reality, but I had one last card to play.

I explained to her how Jill had asked me what I would do in her situation. She quickly interjected to suggest that I would do the same, but I told her that my response to Jill was that if I gave my word to someone I would honour it, despite the fact that it might involve taking pain, and maybe even a considerable amount of pain. My word is my word, I insisted.

There was a long pause, which made me think I might have struck a chord, so I was happy to wait for a few moments. Then I decided it was time to cut to the chase. I asked her what it would take for her to stick with us. Her response was immediate and it seemed considered: 'If you meet me somewhere in the middle then maybe I could accept that.'

I started to calculate in my head: our offer was €420,000, the offer from the Dutch couple was €520,000, so that would mean around €470,000. It was still too much – I was going to have to tell her that our absolute maximum budget was €450,000 but, luckily, she got in before me:

'I would need to get €440,000', she said, firmly.

'Is this net, after agents' fees?'

'Yes, this is the amount I would need to get.'

'Emm ... that's a big jump. If we did raise our offer to this amount, could I be sure that that would be the end of it. No more offers, no more viewings?'

'Yes.'

'I have your word on that? Sorry for persisting, but I don't want the same thing to happen again.'

'That will be it. You have my word.'

'Okay, I can agree to this. But our absolute budget limit is €450,000 so I will need to check with Jill if she will agree to lower her fees. I'm pretty certain she will but I need to be sure.'

In reality I had no idea how Jill was going to react. I suspected she wouldn't be too pleased to have her fees cut by two-thirds, but then again, as things stood, when I last spoke to her she was getting nothing.

So that was it, we were back in business and I was also happy that I managed to part on reasonably good terms with Mrs Sumner. I think she was even happy to hear that I was going to negotiate on the agent's fees, as she said she always felt they were exorbitant anyway.

I went downstairs, buoyed by the outcome of the phone call and eager to share the news with Tanya. As I expected, she was shocked. When Jill had advised us to forget about it she really believed it was over, so she was amazed and thrilled that we had manage to turn it around. Of course, we still had to get Jill to reduce her fees, which was not going to be straightforward. Our budget was €450,000, which would only leave fees of €10,000. This was a long way short of the €35,000 that an agent would normally get from a transaction of this size, but I felt we were in a strong position. Jill had already given up on it so surely €10,000 was better than nothing?

I tried to phone her immediately, as I felt we had some momentum, and I was feeling confident and upbeat after the discussion with Mrs Sumner, and also, of course, because we desperately wanted a resolution. But alas, no answer from

Jill. I eventually got her the next morning. I recounted my discussion with Mrs Sumner and she seemed pleasantly surprised, or maybe completely flabbergasted would be more accurate. I then explained the financial crux and, to my great relief, she accepted this without any discussion. I guess after all the work she had already put into the sale, she was just happy to be getting anything.

I left the office early that day; I just couldn't concentrate on work. At last, we had finally done it. We had got the property we wanted and the move to France was now a reality. It was the beginning of the end of our time in Brussels; the following day we would start making preparations for our new life in France.

6

## *Bah Humbug*

The signing of the *acte* (the final contract) was scheduled for 29 December, and about a week before this we got a serious offer on our house in Brussels. It was unexpected, as our last viewing had been a few weeks earlier and we were not expecting any more developments before Christmas. The following day we received, signed and returned the final contracts from France and we also signed the initial contract for the sale of the house in Brussels. It was almost too good to be true. We ended 2009 as the proud owners of our new property in France, and with our house in Brussels sold for a reasonable price. It had been an eventful year to say the least, but it all seemed to come together in the dying moments.

Christmas 2009 was an opportunity for a deep intake of breath. We could go to Ireland and sit back for a week and savour the prospect of looking forward to the year ahead, to a new adventure and a major new life change. However, in the midst of scoffing mince pies and turkey sandwiches, something started to niggle away at me. I was concerned about our finances. This was my single biggest worry about the move to France. So, on Christmas Day, while everyone was snoozing on the sofa after an enormous lunch, I snuck away for a clandestine rendezvous with my calculator. Later that afternoon, when I failed to show up for Trivial Pursuit, suspicions were aroused, and before long Tanya had hunted me down and reminded me, in no uncertain terms, that it was Christmas. The following day I bounced back with a new plan, which involved hiding my calculator between the pages of a book.

Admittedly, it was a bit sad and desperate, but I had some pressing questions that needed answering. I needed to know what the move to France was going to cost. How much would we net from the sale of the house in Brussels? What would be left over, if anything? Would we need to borrow money? What kind of income could we expect to make from the gîte(s)? What would our cost of living be? Ultimately, what I really wanted to know was, would I still need to work and, if so, how much would I need to earn?

My dream was to be in a position where I didn't have to hold down a regular job. It wasn't that I did not want to work – I just wanted more freedom to choose what kind of work I did, and when.

In the end, the figures looked something like this: the net proceeds from the sale of the house in Brussels, after paying the mortgage and fees, was going to be around €440,000 and our total savings were €60,000. The cost of the house in France, including fees, was €450,000. Taxes would add another €30,000, bringing the total cost to €480,000. The good news was that this meant that we wouldn't need a mortgage, and we would have about €20,000 in the bank to start the renovations. The bad news, however, was that this would not be nearly enough. We did have the option of postponing the renovations for a year or two, to give us the chance to raise the money we needed, but of course that implied the need to continue to hold down a regular job for at least a few more years. With the barn converted to another two gîtes, and doing B&B in the main house, I estimated, optimistically, that we could generate an annual income of around

€28,000. Without a mortgage or any other loan repayments, this, combined with a small amount of other passive income we received, would be enough to fund a modest but comfortable lifestyle.

So, on the whole, it was a mixed picture. The dream life would have to be postponed for a few years until we had the gîtes up and running, but it seemed to be within reach. It would not be an extravagant lifestyle, but we never had and never wanted extravagance. In fact, an important reason for the move was to get away from the high-earning, high-spending culture, where having more money simply meant spending more, but never seemed to buy the most precious and priceless commodity of all – time.

# 7

## Beers and Tears

The early part of the New Year went by in a flash. Nothing very much happened in relation to the house or the move and it was almost the end of January before we started to get serious about the planning and preparations. In early February, with the day of the move fast approaching, we decided to have a little get-together to say goodbye to some good friends we had made in Brussels. My mother and her brother, my uncle Jack, were visiting us at the time, so they came along as well. Our chosen venue for this farewell gig was the Petit Paris, a cosy little bar at the end of the street where we lived. When Tanya, my mother, Jack and I arrived, there were already a few of my work colleagues there, and as the evening wore on, more and more friends and colleagues arrived, until we were eventually about thirty and occupying one whole side of the bar.

It was a very enjoyable evening, and I was really happy that the people we liked most showed up. The majority of them drifted off home shortly after midnight and by 1 a.m. only the rump of the group remained: a true hardcore of about seven, including, naturally, six Irish and one wayward Belgian. This unswerving group then set off for a night-cap at a little all-night bar at the other end of the street, which we had christened The Witches, because, for some strange reason, they never took down their Halloween decorations. The Witches was tiny: at full capacity, it could probably accommodate about twenty people, and it always seemed to attract the oddest bunch of misfits, so it suited us perfectly. We ordered more drinks and then we did what many Irish people do when they have had a few too many – we got into deep conversation about all the things that we never really discussed when sober. This is why the pub is such an important feature of life in Ireland – it's a place for group counselling.

By 4.30 our group of seven had dwindled down to three: my mother, who was still going strong, Uncle Jack and I. The conversation had gotten quite deep by this stage; we were delving into subjects that would normally never have seen the light of day, and, I have to say, I was quite enjoying it. So much so in fact that I suddenly had to urge to tell my two companions how much I loved them. However, as I said these simple but highly charged words, I could feel myself being overcome with emotion. I don't know where it came from, but it was as if I had suddenly tapped into something that had been supressed for a long, long time and there was absolutely nothing I could do to stop it. I think it was a combination of the alcohol, happiness about the move and a kind of catharsis of all the tension and stress that had built up over the previous few months. Moving house is stressful at the best of times, but moving house, moving country and changing jobs, with the added complication of being gazumped at the last moment, brought this to another level altogether.

At first, I tried to mask it and made an attempt to escape to the toilets, but as I tried to get past Jack he grabbed me and pulled me back.

'It's okay, stay where you are, it's alright.'

'I just wanted to say, waaah, that you and Mammy, waaah, waaah …'.

'I know, it's alright …'.

'You always, waaah, waaah, waaah …'.

To this day, I still don't know if they had any idea what was wrong or what I was trying to say. Probably not, as I didn't really know myself, and the next day we were all too hungover and exhausted to even broach the subject. That night did feel like a watershed moment, however, when we closed the door on one chapter of our lives and opened the door to another. From then on, our focus was on France and on looking forward to the challenges and adventures that lay ahead.

## The Rolling Maul

The final signing of the contracts on the sale of our house in Brussels was scheduled for 12 March at 2 p.m., which meant we had to have everything, including ourselves, out of the house before that. In the weeks leading up to this, we had already sent two small truckloads of belongings to the new house, thanks to our soon-to-be neighbour, Lars Carlsson. Lars, who was originally from Sweden, had been helping Mrs Sumner move her things to Cologne, and had kindly agreed to reroute to Brussels on his way back.

On the second of these trips, Tanya and the kids were in Ireland and I was just returning from a rugby match in Paris with some friends from Ireland who were staying overnight. When we got back to Brussels on the Sunday evening, Lars was already waiting outside the house. It was a cold, wet evening and we were all feeling a bit delicate, but thankfully everyone rallied and before long the truck was loaded and we were sitting in front of five strong Belgian beers in the local brassiere. I treated the lads to dinner and a few drinks in return for helping me load the truck, and we then set about interrogating Lars about the place in France. He painted a pretty picture of a rural château with swimming pool, acres of woodland and pastures, a friendly local mayor, a welcoming community and a climate to die for.

The only downside seemed to be some difficult farmer guy called Jacques, but at the time this seemed almost quaint – a move to France just wouldn't be complete without having a difficult farmer for a neighbour. Apparently, Mrs Sumner had allowed Jacques to graze his cows on her land and when it came to the sale there were some issues around relinquishing these rights, and it seemed like he was expecting his rights to be restored as soon as we were in residence. He had even called to Lars' house a few weeks earlier to check that Helena, Lars' partner, would not be putting her horses on the land.

The conversation then turned, as Lars was understandably interested in knowing something about me, his new neighbour, but with the effects of the strong Belgian beer now really taking hold, it was a lost cause. The convoluted stories (complete rubbish of course) of riches acquired from gun-running for the IRA, Irish mafia connections and secret hideaways in the south of France, all accompanied by wild laughter, soon had Lars looking pale and confused. But the paler Lars looked, the more outlandish the stories became. In the end, I'm not sure what he thought, but the next morning he was showing me the kind of reverence that made me suspect he believed at least some of the fiction he had been fed, despite my protestations to the contrary. He also seemed quite anxious to get on the road, and even decided to eat his breakfast in the truck, rather than join us around a cardboard box in the kitchen. As I accompanied him to the truck, I sought to reassure him that I was a nice guy, but as I listened to myself speak, it started to sound like I was trying to hide something. I decided to shut up. He would soon get to know us and, hopefully, he would see then that all this was just a joke.

## Falling into a Black Hole

Two weeks later, we were still moving the last of our belongings from the house. It was the day of the signing so we had to get everything out by 2 p.m. At about 11.30 that morning

I went to drop back our Sky digital box to the rental shop. With so much to do that day, I was in a rush. On top of that, I was a bit stressed about everything that still had to be done at the house, so my mind and the car were racing.

As I turned onto the street where the shop was located, all I could see was a long row of cars stretched out on either side; there wasn't a parking space in sight. I started to drive slowly down the street, hoping to see a gap but it didn't look good. About halfway down the street I finally saw an opening on the opposite side of the street. As I got closer I noticed that it was in front of a lock-up garage, but there was no 'no parking' sign on the garage door and, in any case, I wasn't going to be very long in the shop, so I decided to go for it.

I swung the car around in the middle of the road and as I completed the turn, I suddenly noticed that there was a sheet of what looked like plywood on the ground in the space where I was planning to park. I didn't take too much notice of it at first, as I had seen things like this left on the street before and there were no signs indicating any danger, so I continued on. As I drove onto the plywood everything seemed fine, but then, as the right wheel rolled into the centre of the sheet I heard a cracking sound, and suddenly the car began to lean to one side and sink into the ground, deeper and deeper, until eventually the front of the car was leaning at a 45-degree angle and the front right wheel was suspended in mid-air over a large hole.

It felt like slow motion, but in fact it all happened quite quickly, and I had no time to drive forward or backwards. I sat there feeling helpless and a little embarrassed. Passers-by looked on in amusement, and bewilderment, as I crouched down in the car, shaking my head in disgust. I first tried to restart the car to see if it would move, but it was going nowhere, so I got out, just in case the whole thing fell into the hole. I then called the emergency breakdown service, but the girl on the other end of the line seemed a bit perplexed. 'Your car is in a hole? ... On the side of the street?'

It did all sound a bit strange, but I insisted I needed a crane, and quickly. She said it would be there in thirty minutes. I called Tanya, who was expecting me home shortly, and tried to reassure her that I was unhurt and, more importantly, would be back in time for the signing. After fifty minutes of waiting, the truck finally arrived, just as I was beginning to feel the early symptoms of hypothermia kicking in. It looked small, with only a very small crane on the back. The driver, a Groucho Marx look-alike, jumped out, with a wry grin on his face. He didn't say anything, but I knew what he was thinking. He took a few minutes to assess the situation and then he announced that he would have to call a bigger truck, with a bigger crane. It would be there in thirty minutes, he assured me, and before I could say anything he was gone.

I stood on the side of the street, cold, perplexed and helpless. If I had been superstitious I would have seriously reconsidered the move to France at this stage, as it certainly looked like someone, somewhere was trying to tell us something, but I'm not, and so the struggle continued. By now it was clear that I wasn't going to make the signing, so I phoned Tanya again and asked her to see if she could postpone it until 4 p.m.

Another hour passed before the big truck finally arrived, with its industrial-sized crane. It turned more than a few heads as it drove down the street, and when it stopped beside me and my sunken car, I just wanted the ground to swallow me up as well. This time another equally animated driver emerged, grinning from ear to ear. In the corner of my eye, I could also see two workmen peering around the corner a little further down the street. When I drove into the hole, they had been standing nearby, but by the time I got out of the car they had mysteriously disappeared – possibly something to do with the fact that they probably should have covered the hole with something a little stronger than cardboard.

The crane worked a treat, and within minutes the car was swinging gracefully through the air. I looked on from the footpath, trying my best to blend in with the other bystanders. Once it was on the ground, the man from the garage checked it over and, fortunately, there didn't seem to be any major damage. Within a few minutes I was back on the road. I still had the Sky box on the back seat, but at least I had the car back, so we still had a fighting chance of making it to France the following day.

When I got back to the house it was already 3.30 p.m., so I picked Tanya up on the street and we continued on to the *notaire*'s office. We arrived outside the office at exactly 3.58 p.m. Tanya ran ahead, while I looked for somewhere to park, and tried to compose myself before following her in. But I hadn't even gotten out of the car when I saw Tanya coming running back out of the *notaire*'s office in a state of panic.

Oh no, what could have gone wrong now?

'Start the car … they've moved the signing to the office of the buyer's *notaire*. She said they e-mailed us yesterday. The secretary is ringing ahead to tell them we're on the way.'

So off we went, relieved that we were still going to make it, but also slightly jittery from the combination of exhaustion and excitement. 'You couldn't make it up if you tried', I observed, already sensing the makings of a book taking shape. When we finally arrived at the other *notaire*'s office, there was a spontaneous round of applause and cheering as we entered the room. I felt like a right gobshite – the story of the car in the hole had obviously gotten around. Eventually, when the drama died down, we finally got around to the signing, and, thankfully, there were no further hiccups. With the contracts signed, we were on the move again, back to the house this time, to remove the last of our stuff. We had assured the new owners that we would be gone by 6 p.m.

§

At 7 p.m., as I made my way down the stairs with yet another large box of I don't know what, I could see a silhouette at the front door. It looked like Marcus, the new owner. I wanted to turn back and hide upstairs, but it was too late; he was already in before I could make my move.

'Ah, hi there', I bellowed, doing my best to look pleased to see him.

I could see Marcus' face drop but, like me, he managed to cover it up.

'Oh, hi, you're still here then. Should we come back later?'

'No, no, not at all, come on in. We're just taking the last few things. We'll be gone in no time', I insisted, knowing full well that we were going to be there for at least another hour or two.

Marcus was followed in the door by his wife, Nora, and her parents, all carrying trays of beautifully prepared canapés. Marcus himself was brandishing an expensive-looking bottle of champagne and some glasses. Obviously they had planned a little celebration, and I was pretty sure we weren't part of the plan. They did invite us to join them, but we politely declined and pressed on with the job of trying to get the hell out of there. At this stage, we couldn't fit another nanoparticle into the car, and having given what we could to neighbours and friends, we were now taking the extreme measure of leaving what remained on the street outside the house. This was common practice in Brussels, to leave unwanted items on the side of the street. Normally, within a few hours, most of it would be picked up by people who seemed to just drive around the city, waiting to pounce on such opportunities.

By 9.30 p.m., everything was out of the house, with a considerable amount of it in a pile on the street outside. We spent that night with our English neighbours, Simon and Lucy, who cooked us a beautiful farewell dinner, and we drank and talked late into the night.

## On the Road

I woke early the next morning. It felt nice, almost liberating, to wake up in someone else's house, having left life's responsibilities and stresses elsewhere. It reminded me of when I was a student at university and the feeling I had the day after finishing the end-of-year exams. In the midst of this dreamy moment, I was suddenly jolted back to reality when Astrid stormed through the door looking for her dodo. Okay, I wasn't a young, carefree student anymore, but it still felt exciting.

After breakfast, we loaded up the last few remaining items. The very last thing to go into the car was Nipper, our cat, who had thankfully reappeared after going AWOL the night before. To prepare him for the long journey ahead, Tanya gave him a large bar of some kind of sedative-infused cat treat, which he was certainly going to need, especially if he had any kind of claustrophobic tendencies, as his small cage just about fit into the remaining space in the boot, and it was completely surrounded by bags, cases, pillows and duvets.

'Bon voyage, Nipper', I said, as I slammed closed the boot, consummating his incarceration.

And then it was time to say our goodbyes. I hate goodbyes, but if it has to happen then I prefer to be the one leaving. The people leaving have usually made a conscious decision to leave, and there is always something exciting about leaving behind the familiar to embark on something new, but there's still a certain sense of loss when you leave people behind and close a chapter in your life that you know won't be repeated.

As we pulled away, a small group huddled together to wave us off. It had taken us eight years to build up this close group of friends and it felt to me, and probably to them as well, as if we were deserting them. As we drove on down the street, the car laden to the ground with the last of our belongings, and the two kids looking a little stunned in the back seat, the real impact of the move struck home with me for the first time. We had cut all our ties now – friends, house, career – and we were leaving behind a secure and comfortable existence in Brussels for something new and unknown. Things hadn't been perfect there. If they had we would not have wanted to leave. But are things ever perfect? And there was a lot that was right about the life we were now saying goodbye to: we had a nice house in a good area; we had nice neighbours and friends; I had a good job; there was a good school nearby; and Ned loved his teacher and was already getting settled and making friends. I crossed my fingers and hoped that we were doing the right thing.

As we continued on towards the motorway, the initial sense of shock began to subside and the mood in the car started to lift. Then Tanya opened the bag of pastries we stopped off to buy on our way out of the city and we all perked up even more. The sun was shining, a new life lay ahead – it was a time to be happy and look forward.

# 8

# The New Life

We had decided to break the journey so that we would arrive at the house during daylight, so later that evening we stopped off at a roadside hotel, just on the outskirts of Limoges. It was a relief that we had gotten that far without any major problems and that we had only about three hours driving left the next morning. I opened the boot to find Nipper spread-eagled in his cage. At first I thought he was dead but on closer examination I noticed he was still breathing, and I could hear a faint snoring sound. When I removed the cage from the boot he came to momentarily, lifted his head, looked around, and then flopped back down again, poleaxed. We rose early the next morning and, having re-charged Nipper with some of the good stuff, we were on the road again by 9 a.m. A few hours later we pulled off the motorway again, just outside Cahors. We decided to drive into the town to have a look around and pick up some essentials.

Cahors is the capital of the Lot department. An impressive, medieval town of about 25,000 people, it nestles in a loop of the River Lot. The centre of the town dates back to medieval times, with narrow streets and tall buildings. The main thoroughfare, Rue Gambetta, is more recent and grander, typical of the boulevards you see in most provincial towns in France. One of the town's greatest treasures is the medieval Pont Valentré, a magical fairy-tale bridge that crosses the river to the west of the town.

After the long journey, it really felt like we were in a strange place, far away from anything familiar. But for its part, the Lot was doing everything it could to make us feel welcome. It was only mid-March but the sun was shining brightly and it was warm, around 25 degrees Celsius. In the bright sunlight, everything looked stunning: the historic, medieval centre of Cahors, surrounded on three sides by the peaceful meandering River Lot, and beyond the river, as far as the eye could see, thousands of hectares of rolling, wooded countryside.

We parked in the centre of town, planning on buying what we needed in the nearby covered market. However, just as we approached the entrance to the market the gates swung closed – an early reminder that we were now in rural France. Cahors is a typical provincial French town – it holds on to traditions, and it does not, for example, tolerate 24-hour shopping, all-night bars or Sunday afternoon trading. The pace of life is different, and everything, including commerce, revolves around lifestyle, and not vice versa. Such vestiges of a bygone era, which have all but vanished in most parts of the Western world, have found a stronghold in the Lot. In one way we were quite happy about this, as it almost enforced a certain work–life balance, which is what we were looking for. But it took a considerable amount of getting used to, and over the following months I lost track of the number of times I was caught out by the 12–2 p.m. lunch break, having driven the 9 kilometres to Prayssac or the 18 kilometres to Cahors for something I urgently needed to fight off an invasion of insects or to fix some kind of power tool that I hadn't even heard of a few months earlier. It takes a while to learn to live with these differences but, once you do, I'm convinced it's for the better. A definite benefit has to be the fact that families and friends have time to sit and eat together every day, and to spend at least one whole day of the week together, without the intrusion of work or the compulsion to go shopping.

With the market closed, we sat down outside a small café and ate a delicious four-course *menu de jour*, including wine, for a very modest €10 for adults and €6 for children. And so, with full bellies and the beginnings of a suntan, we set off on the last leg of the journey. The closer we got the more excited and anxious we became. What kind of condition was the house going to be in? Would we see faults that we had not noticed before? Would we be disappointed and wish we could turn around and go back to the house we no longer owned in Brussels?

Finally, at 2.40 p.m. on Sunday, 14 March 2010, we arrived at 'the new house'. As we crept up the drive, any last-minute doubts we might have had were quickly dispelled. Everything looked more or less as we had remembered. In fact, the tree-lined avenue looked even more inviting than before. We parked the car directly in front of the house and got out to take in the surroundings. We stood in silence, absorbing every little detail. There was a lot to take in. Then a loud voice came booming from somewhere to the rear of the car.

'Welcome, welcome, new neighbours!'

Lars' familiar face was a welcome sight, and his joyous welcome helped to take our minds off the fact that we were probably a little overwhelmed. He led us up the steps, onto the terrace, and pushed open the magnificent old oak front door. Suddenly everything felt right again. As soon as we walked inside, I got that familiar warm feeling. It was a beautiful house, a home, and this time it really was ours.

In the midst of all the excitement, I found it difficult to pay attention to Lars, who was trying his best to convey some important information about how to turn on the water, what utility companies we needed to contact and so on. He brought me down to the basement to show me how to use the heating system, but I was completely distracted and, to

Lars' frustration, not really in the mood for a lesson on the finer points of oil burners. Anyway, it was 25 degrees Celsius outside. Surely we wouldn't need to worry about that until the following winter? Recognising that we hadn't the slightest interest in acquiring any knowledge that might be in some way useful to us, Lars gave up the ghost and suggested that he would leave us to get settled in. But he promised to return later that evening with his partner, Helena, for a welcome toast.

In the meantime, we continued our exploration of the house, opening all the shutters as we went. It seemed in good condition, especially as it had been uninhabited for most of the winter. Okay, there were a few thousand dead insects of various sizes and shapes lying around, and quite a few live ones as well, but nothing that a good vacuuming wouldn't sort out.

As there was very little furniture in the house, we decided to set up base in two downstairs bedrooms, at least until we got the beds and other furniture assembled upstairs. The downstairs bedrooms were basic, with dated, emerald-coloured carpets and white walls that badly needed some freshening up. But they seemed reasonably clean and there was an en suite, which was in good working order, even though it too was dated, with a shocking pink washbasin and a purple toilet – the 70s have a lot to answer for.

We had just about got the sleeping arrangements organised when the doorbell rang. I could hear Tanya opening the door and then the sound of Lars' familiar voice again. I went to join them, curious also to meet Helena. They were both standing by the table when I entered. Helena turned to greet me. She was tall and pretty and came across as being a bit shy, but seemed very nice. Lars was not so shy, and if anything was becoming more boisterous every time I met him. He spoke loudly and, spurred on by a couple of glasses of wine, he was soon giving us quite a gritty account of our new neighbourhood and neighbours. During this sometimes quite open and frank monologue, I noticed out of the side of my eye that every now and then Helena would give Lars a piercing stare, and he would suddenly pause and declare, 'I should stop, I talk too much', before continuing on again with his colourful depiction of life in a sleepy French village.

Eventually, after one really cold, penetrating look from Helena, Lars jumped to his feet and announced that they should go, that we had a lot to do. I didn't argue with him – we had a lot to do – but it was also interesting to get an insider's account of life in our new community, and to learn more about our neighbours. There was one in particular Lars drew special attention to: Jacques the farmer, whom he had already mentioned when we met in Brussels. But on this occasion he went a step further: 'Be careful', he warned. 'Farmers have a lot of rights here when it comes to land.' On the whole, however, Lars and Helena seemed happy and I got the impression they really liked the area.

After they left we continued with the unpacking. In particular, we were keen to locate some cooking and eating utensils, as it was now well past dinner time. I found the cutlery, but the plates were in a different box, which we suspected was at the bottom of a large pile we had just stacked in the living room. I started to re-pile the boxes on the other side of the room, but when I finally reached the bottom box there were still no plates. For me, it's the little things like this that make moving stressful. I can negotiate all the big hurdles, like a car being driven into a hole, or legal or financial complications, but then some little thing comes along, like a missing plate, or not being able to find a particular piece of clothing, and I'm knocked for six. Tanya insists it's a man thing: that all men get moody and contrary when they're hungry or when they can't find something that's usually right in front of their noses. She might be right. I've certainly proven the theory correct on more than one occasion.

While I was desperately rummaging around in a pile of boxes like a half-starved animal, the doorbell rang again. Ten seconds later, Tanya came running into the living room with a look of horror on her face.

'It's the farmer, he's here. It's Jacques, the farmer Lars told us about. What are we going to do?'

'It's okay, don't worry. I'm sure he's fine', I said, trying to maintain a sense of calm. 'I'll go and talk to him. Where is he?'

In the hungry state I was in, I was no mood to be intimidated by farmer Jacques, so while his timing was bad in one way, in another way it couldn't have been better.

'He went walking around the side of the house. Be careful; you heard what Lars said about him.'

I walked purposefully around the side of the house and saw Jacques standing in the garden, pacing back and forth with his head down. He was around fifty, average height and heavily built, like a man who was well used to physical work. His thick black hair belied his age, but up close his skin was tough and weather-beaten and his dark, deep-set eyes were slightly unnerving. I decided it was best not to make assumptions and to see if I could get things off on a friendly footing.

'Bonjour monsieur', I said, extending my hand.

'What are you going to do with the land?', he snapped, in a strong local French dialect.

I smiled and kept my hand extended, determined to leave it there for as long as it took. He stared at me, like he was assessing me, but eventually conceded and shook my hand, albeit very limply. He then muttered something under his breath, repeating his demand to know what we were doing with the land.

'We just arrived a couple of hours ago', I said, calmly. 'We have a lot to think about and we haven't decided yet what we want to do with the land. We'd like to get some animals but we haven't decided on anything yet.'

I wanted to make it clear to him that the land wasn't going to be available to him, but at the same time I really had no idea at this stage what we were going to do with it, so I didn't want to be too precise.

'What kind of animals?'

'As I said, we've just arrived. We haven't decided yet. We need to think about it, to see what the land is suitable for and decide then.'

'Horses? Sheep?', he persisted.

I started to feel like I was being evasive, trying to cover something up, until I remembered that I didn't actually have to tell him anything. It was none of his business, and the truth of it was that we did want animals but we hadn't decided what kind.

'Maybe, we'll have to see. I come from a farm in Ireland, so I know something about farming, but I want to get to know the land here before we decide anything', I responded, taking the opportunity to let him know that I wasn't a complete greenhorn. He looked away and started to pace again. He didn't seem pleased with the direction of the conversation.

'Where would I go to buy farm animals around here?', I enquired, trying to keep things amicable.

'To buy animals? Oh, *boef*!', he puffed, throwing his hands up in exasperation. 'There are markets in Gourdon and Duravel and Cahors', he said dismissingly. 'What do you want to buy: horses, sheep?'

'We'll have to see. I'm just interested to know about the markets', I said sternly, extending my hand again. It was time to bring our discussion to a close. He reluctantly shook my hand again, looking away and muttering something else under this breath about coming back, which was really not what I wanted to hear. He turned and walked off without saying anything else.

'*Au revoir*', I called after him.

Back inside, not wishing to alarm Tanya, I told her it had all been fairly civil and that I had explained to him that we would be using the land ourselves. But in reality, I knew this wasn't the last we were going to hear from Jacques.

It was now past 8 p.m., so we decided to abandon the search for plates and resorted instead to eating from saucepans. As we had no television to crash out in front of, an early night beckoned, and it was certainly needed. It had been a long day and we hadn't had much sleep for a few days. Despite this, I still didn't sleep well on this first night. I had too many things on my mind; two in particular were unsettling me.

The first was the fact that we were in a new house. Well, actually it was an old house, a very old house, and because of that it felt a little bit eerie. Everything was unfamiliar, and it didn't feel like it was ours just yet. I had the feeling of someone else's presence. It took me a couple of months to get over this. I had to get to know every room in the house intimately before they started to feel safe and familiar, and before the ghosts of the previous owners were finally banished.

The second thing on my mind was fire. I have this thing about fires. Every house I have ever lived in I have always had to satisfy myself that there is a credible escape route in the event of a fire. I had become even more fastidious about this since we had children, as now I also needed to know we would get them out safely. I had gone through the whole thing in my head, but there was only one stairs and the first floor of the house was just too high off the ground to jump. So, if we couldn't make it down the stairs we were in trouble. In the weeks that followed I investigated all kinds of solutions, including inflatable slides (like they use on aeroplanes, but I couldn't find anyone selling these), fire escape ladders, and I even considered erecting a system of pulleys, with a steel rope running from the bedroom window to a nearby tree. In the end, I settled for a rope ladder, which I put in a drawer near Astrid's bedroom. I also installed smoke alarms and fire extinguishers. It wasn't the complete answer, but it was some reassurance.

§

The next morning, I got up early, put on the same clothes as the day before, as I couldn't find anything else, and set about looking for some cereal bowls. Shortly after we finished breakfast, all eating from the same bowl, I had a call from one of my clients in Brussels – there was some urgent writing and editing work to be done and they were checking my availability. In truth, I wasn't available. We had a mountain of boxes to unpack, furniture to be assembled and walls to be painted; on top of that, we had no internet access. But I really wanted to get off to a good start and to prove that having a freelance contractor based in the south of France was workable, so I agreed to write an entire section of a new guidebook and edit the whole document by the following Friday. Utter madness!

As soon as I hung up I started to panic. My biggest worry was how I was going to organise internet access, which I absolutely needed to do this work. I grabbed the keys of the car and as I stormed through the kitchen I explained to Tanya that I had to go to Cahors, urgently, to see if I could sort out internet access.

I raced out the gate, down through the village of Martassac, and on towards the main road to Cahors. I was stressed and rushing, but I still couldn't help noticing the beauty of the villages and the countryside along the route. It was captivating, almost spellbinding, and for just a few moments I completely forgot about work and internet access and just enjoyed the scenery. Twenty minutes later I arrived in Cahors. There was a lively atmosphere in the town that morning, with lots of people on the streets and plenty of traffic. Without too much searching, I found an internet provider on the main street. He sold me a satellite dish, a wifi box and a few other gadgets and told me that someone would contact me in the next couple of weeks to arrange to erect the dish and set up the box. I looked at him curiously, so he repeated it, assuming I didn't understand. I could feel the blood rushing into my face and it probably looked as if I was about to blow a fuse. I wasn't, of course, I was just shocked, worried, disappointed and frustrated, all at the same time, and stuck for the appropriate French words to express it all.

'Do you need it urgently?', he enquired, suddenly striking a more helpful tone.

I found my voice again. 'Yes, today would be good. Is that not possible?'

He went back to his computer screen and brought up the details of an *installateur*. I peered over his shoulder as he wrote a short e-mail.

'I've asked the installer to contact you as soon as possible to make an appointment. Normally, he should call you in the next couple of days.'

'Is it not possible for me to call him?', I pleaded.

'I'm afraid not. We are not authorised to give out the numbers of the installers.'

'Okay, no problem', I said, as I turned and left the shop, suddenly appearing much more understanding. What the shop assistant hadn't noticed was that while he was writing the e-mail I had managed to memorise the mobile number of the *installateur*, which I could see on the screen. As soon as I was outside the shop I called him, implying that the shop had provided his number so I could arrange for an urgent installation. From experience, I knew it wasn't a good idea to wait for a service provider to call you, and this was probably truer in rural France than anywhere. After a lengthy discussion, he said the very earliest he could be there was the end of the week, so we agreed on Saturday morning; at least it was an improvement on a couple of weeks.

In the meantime, deadlines were looming large and I had no choice but to find a temporary solution. A nice lady in the tourist office gave me a list of three places in the town centre with public internet access. The closest was the Hotel Amelie, so I made my way there, with my laptop under my arm. The hotel was located close to the marketplace. It was small and a bit rundown looking from the outside, but that was the least of my worries; I had work to do. Inside, I was met by a very friendly lady. She was a good-looking woman: probably mid-forties, well groomed, slender, with shoulder-length blonde hair and a very elegant-looking black dress. It was a sharp contrast to the hotel's shabby façade. I ordered a coffee and asked her if there was internet access.

*'Mais bien sur monsieur* [but of course sir]', she said, smiling. She explained that the reception was better at the back of the building, in a little room just off the hotel reception. She led the way, insisting on carrying my coffee. En route, she must have asked me a thousand questions, all in quick succession, only leaving me enough time for one-syllable responses. Halfway through this interrogation, as we passed by the door of the kitchen, she told me that her ex-husband ('I am now divorced, you see', she smiled at me again, eyes fluttering) was American, and immediately switched to speaking English. By the time we got to the little room at the back, she had shared most of the highlights of her life, and she probably knew the first 2 per cent of lots of different bits of mine.

I installed myself on a very low-set sofa in front of an equally low-set coffee table. It wasn't the most comfortable working arrangement, but there was no other furniture in the room and I was desperate to check my e-mails. I proceeded to start up my laptop while she stood nearby, looking on in admiration and admitting that she herself wasn't very good with computers and that I would have to show her some 'tricks'. I smiled, glanced fleetingly in her direction, and then quickly turned my attention back to the computer.

'I should introduce myself. My name is Miranda', she said, pushing her hand towards me. Strangely, she presented me with the back of her hand, so I wasn't sure if she expected me to shake it or kiss it, but I opted for shaking.

'Nice to meet you Miranda, I'm Eamon.'

'Eamon, wow; what a lovely name.'

'It's Irish. I come from Ireland originally', I explained.

'Oh, so you are Irish. Wow, that's nice! What's it like in Ireland then?'

'Well, it rains a lot', I responded politely, maintaining my fixation on the computer, hoping that she would not probe any further.

After another five minutes, she finally had the good sense to leave me alone. I had 35 unread messages in my inbox and most of them needed an urgent response. I was going to be there for longer than I intended, so I phoned Tanya. Just before I hung up, Miranda looked around the door again.

'Do you want some more dear?', she enquired, as she leaned over me to pick up my coffee cup.

'No thanks, that's fine for now, thank you', I whispered, holding my hand over the mouthpiece. She grimaced and winked at me, and then placed a finger over her lips, signalling that we needed to be quiet, as if we had some shared secret. As she turned to leave, I took my hand off the mouthpiece again.

'Just let me know if you need me for anything else, Eamon dear', she bellowed.

'Who's that?'

'Oh, it's just the woman from the hotel. I'll explain later.'

'You better!'

As I left the hotel about two hours later, I explained to Miranda that I might have to come back for a few more days, as I was waiting for my internet access to be sorted out.

'You're welcome here any time, Eamon', she said in a soft voice.

That evening Tanya was busy with the kids and Miranda was never mentioned. It was a relief, as I hadn't the energy to explain, nor did I really know what to say, although I knew Miranda was flirting with me and I feared some awkward moments in the following days.

The next morning I arrived at the hotel just after 9 a.m. Miranda was already behind the bar, looking and sounding every bit as spritely as the day before.

'*Bonjour mon cheri*, and how are you today?'

'Fine thanks Miranda. Is it alright if I use your internet again?'

'Of course dear, for as long as you like. You go on through and I'll bring you down some coffee.'

I made my way to the same room as the day before and got busy on my computer as quickly as I could. A few minutes later, Miranda arrived with the coffee. This time she closed the door behind her. I could see that she had freshened up a little in the ten minutes since I had last seen her. Her perfume was also stronger and I'm pretty sure that another button had come undone on her sparkling white cotton blouse.

'Thanks very much. Is it okay if I pay you for everything on the way out this evening?', I enquired, looking out from under my eyebrows.

'Or you could pay me now?', Miranda retorted, in a soft voice.

I was caught off guard by this. My immediate assumption was that she wanted the money straight away, but when I looked up I could tell from her expression that she meant something entirely different. She was a good-looking woman, and there was a kind of a cheeky, fun side to her that I liked, but I didn't need any more complications in my life, and I had a mountain of work to do. Fortunately, at the end of the half-second it took for all this to flash through my overloaded brain, I could hear someone calling Miranda. I seized the opportunity.

'I think someone's looking for you?'

'Oh, it's just Theo, my son', she said dismissively.

But the call got louder and eventually she had to respond. She opened the door just wide enough to call out to Theo, who then came barging down the hallway and proceeded to push his way through the door. Theo was about seventeen or eighteen and looked a bit like a young Jimi Hendrix, with dark skin and a big mane of black, fuzzy hair. He didn't look anything like Miranda, so I guessed that he must have taken after his dad.

Miranda introduced me as her Irish friend, as if we had known each other for years. I extended my hand, which Theo attached himself to with way too much enthusiasm. He seemed like a nice lad, but I was a little bit uneasy about where the whole thing was going, or what she might have told him.

The sooner I get out of here the better, I thought. Miranda was on some kind of mission and it made me uncomfortable. The best thing to do was to just try to keep my head down. That was easier said than done, however, and the rest of the week went on pretty much as it started, with regular visits from Miranda and few more awkward moments along the way. At one point I did contemplate moving to one of the two other places in town with internet access, but one only opened in the afternoons and the other seemed to be permanently overrun with students, and it didn't look like the kind of place you could spend the entire day. So I was stuck with Miranda. But in the end, I survived. Well, almost. When I was leaving the hotel on the Friday evening, I told Miranda that I wouldn't be back the week after as we were having the internet installed at home the following day, but I said I would call in for a coffee sometime. She walked out from around the bar and approached me, with a sad, dejected look on her face.

'Be sure you do come back', she insisted, as she put her arms out to embrace me. I moved forward to kiss her on the cheek but as I did she turned her head and planted her lips firmly on mine. Before I knew what was happening she had turned and was walking back to the bar. I walked outside; the cool evening air was a welcome antidote!

# 9

## Strangers in a Strange Land

At around 2.30 p.m. on Saturday afternoon the internet guy arrived, and he wasted no time in getting started on installing our television and internet system. It was a nice sunny day; in fact the sun had been shining every day since we arrived, which we were now beginning to accept as the norm for this part of France.

After much banging and rattling on the roof, where he was installing the satellite dish, he turned his attention to the television and wifi box in the living room. There was no signal on either, so he went back onto the roof to change the orientation of the dish, but still nothing. He went back up again, and again and again; he must have been up and down about ten times, but still there was no signal. He even tried a few different satellite dishes, but it made no difference. After a few hours of this he came into the kitchen, where Tanya and I were busily unpacking more boxes, threw his hands up in the air and made tractor sounds through his lips. It didn't look good.

'I just can't get a signal. I don't understand it; I've never had this problem before. I've tried everything – the box, the dish, the cable, but they all seem fine. I don't understand it

.... I'll come back next week with a new dish. That's all I can think of.'

This wasn't the news I wanted to hear, but I was satisfied that the poor man had tried everything and he looked like he was close to tears, so I didn't want to make a fuss. It was almost 7 p.m. at this stage and he should have been finished hours earlier.

'When next week?', I enquired, trying hard to contain the sense of panic that was overtaking me.

'I will have to look at my schedule, but maybe Wednesday?'

'WEDNESDAY?! Can you not come before then? I really need the internet for my work; it's very important.'

I knew he had tried everything, and had gone way beyond the call of duty, but there was just no way I was going back to the Hotel Amelie again the following week. He had to do something before Wednesday. He got his diary and checked but he insisted he couldn't do it before Wednesday. Seeing my disappointment, he suggested that he would try one more time before he left. He headed back onto the roof and there was the familiar banging and rattling and then he arrived back down into the living room. Miraculously, there was a signal this time. It was very faint but it was still a signal. It took a few more trips up and down the stairs to improve the reception, but an hour later we had television and internet.

A great weight was lifted from my shoulders and when the work was done I insisted that the hero of the hour join me in a celebratory Duvel, a very strong Belgian beer that I had developed a penchant for during our time in Brussels. He agreed, and we chatted away for a while about football, Ireland and our mutual love of good beer. As it was late, I told him that if he didn't want to finish the beer I wouldn't be offended, so he politely moved the jungle juice to the centre of the table and headed off on his merry way. I waved him off from the terrace and watched as the van disappeared down the lane. As I turned to go back into the house, the sound of screeching brakes and tyres skidding on gravel stopped me in my tracks. I ran down the lane to get a closer look and found two white vans pushed right up against each other. Fortunately, there didn't seem to be any damage. It seemed like the merry technician had narrowly escaped a head-on collision with a Renault van, which just happened to be coming in the gate as he was on his way out.

Seeing as everything appeared to be okay, I didn't intervene. I strolled back towards the house to wait for whomever it was in the white van who was paying us a visit at such a late hour. It didn't seem to be farmer Jacques, or at least it wasn't the car he was driving on his first visit. Maybe it would be someone nice, I thought. The white van approached at speed and, before it came to a stop, the driver's door was already open and a large, burly-looking man jumped out and looked at me with a wide, toothy grin. He bid me a nice evening, and then jumped back in and pulled on the handbrake. He reappeared, still smiling, and walked towards me with his hand outstretched.

'Alagcjbjmknhangcljkjnknprtangmjgangdlbfdlnjang, ldfjblang', he said.

I asked him if he could repeat it. It wasn't much clearer to me the second time, but I did manage to make out that his name was Alain something, and that he was a member of the local hunters' association. He looked about 55, but he could have been anywhere between 45 and 65. I found it difficult to tell the ages of the people living in this part of France. Alain was balding and had a big handlebar moustache under his nose, which hid a large part of his face. But underneath, his skin was sallow and he had a youthful complexion, so he could easily have been much younger than I thought.

I had been expecting his visit. Lars had briefed me in some considerable detail about the hunters during our first meeting in Brussels, so I knew why he had come. He was friendly and jovial; his big frame shaking all over every time he laughed. He looked overjoyed when I told him we were Irish, throwing his hands up in delight. He then burst into another cacophony of words, only some of which I could decipher:

'Fantastique … rugby … passion … fantastique … coeur [placing his hand on his heart] … O'Driscoll … fantastique …', all of which was intermingled with explosions of laughter and cheering. During this discussion, which admittedly was rather one-sided, I started to recognise some of the nuances of the local accent, such as the fact that everything seemed to end in 'ang'. I didn't understand everything he said, but it all sounded good and positive so I just smiled and nodded in affirmation. After five or ten minutes of this bonhomie, Alain suddenly took on a more serious, even slightly persecuted look.

'About the hunting', he said, his gaze shifting from me to the ground, where his large left foot was tapping nervously on the gravel. 'You know … the members of the association will only hunt in areas where the landowners have given their permission', he pleaded, looking decidedly uncomfortable.

I took no pleasure in watching a grown man in such a predicament, so I interjected to assure him that we didn't have a problem with hunting on our land. In truth, I wasn't overly enthusiastic about it. It wasn't that I was against hunting per se, as I knew wild boar and deer numbers needed to be kept under control, but I had some concerns about the safety aspects, and what danger we might be exposed to while walking on our own land. However, we had been forewarned by Lars that if we said no to the hunters, we would be effectively ostracised from the local community. Most of the men in the area hunted. It was part of their way of life, and also an important part of the local culture, with many local events and activities organised by the hunters' association.

So, in the interests of ingratiating ourselves with our new neighbours, I acquiesced. And there was no time for having second thoughts either, as no sooner were the words out of my mouth than Alain's white van was on the move again, reversing back down the drive, with Alain still only half in, struggling to gain control of the car and say goodbye at the same time. I watched from the house as he fled down the lane, still wrestling with the car, which was swaying dangerously from side to side.

It was a brief but strange encounter, which I would soon come to understand was not so unusual when you meet someone for the first time in this little rural neighbourhood where, understandably, caution is well exercised. Having said that, most of the local people we met were very friendly, and during our first few weeks in the area a number of them dropped in to welcome us. Part of the motivation, I'm sure, was to give us the once over, and we didn't really have a problem with that, but we did wonder sometimes how well we were standing up to such scrutiny.

The local community was so mixed, from youngish Swedes, to sophisticated middle-aged Parisians, to elderly wealthy Dutch people, to English people of all coats and classes, and of course the born and bred locals, so it was very difficult to be all things to all people. All we could do was be ourselves and hope for the best. However, the big opportunity to meet the community, and to be met and vetted, was just around the corner, as a couple of days after the visit from Alain we received an invitation to the annual hunters' ball, which was due to take place a few weeks later. We had heard from Lars that this was an event not to be missed, so we were delighted to be invited, and so soon after our arrival.

I went to bed feeling more upbeat that night. I was encouraged by that fact that the first French workman we had dealings with was so friendly and obliging, and we seemed to have gotten off to a good start with the hunters. Things were looking up, or so it seemed. Little did I know, however, that my sense of contentment was to be short-lived, as lurking around the corner was a succession of events that you just couldn't have made up. If I had locked myself in a dark room and tried to imagine all the unsavoury things that could have bedevilled us when we moved to France, I still would not have foreseen what was coming next.

## Ashes to Ashes

The day after the invitation arrived from the hunters' association, halfway through our second week in France, the weather broke. The temperature dropped at least 10 degrees and the sun basically disappeared for about six weeks. According to local knowledge, this was unheard of. At first we didn't take much notice. We had had a really nice first week and a half, so a little pause in the weather was only to be expected, especially as it was still only March. And anyway, being Irish, we instinctively expected bad weather, it was only natural. But after a few weeks of non-stop rain and cold, it started to get depressing, even by Irish standards. What made it worse was the fact that in Ireland, unusually, the weather was absolutely fantastic, or at least that's what we were being told by family and friends. I'm pretty sure they were exaggerating, a not uncommon Irish trait, but we still couldn't help feeling like we had gotten a raw deal.

During this prolonged wintry period we also made an important new discovery about the house – it was almost impossible to heat! There was a good oil-fired central heating system and plenty of radiators, but with bare stone walls and mostly single-glazed windows, the heat was escaping as quickly as we could produce it. On the plus side, we now had internet access, but as I sat in my quaint and characterful little office in the east tower, trying to complete my assignments, my fingers and face were taking on a bluish hue that was starting to become a permanent feature. Meanwhile, Tanya and the kids had taken to huddling around the open fire downstairs, trying to extract a small portion of the heat before it escaped up the metre-wide chimney.

§

In early April, my sister Fiona, her husband and their two children came to visit. They were our first visitors and we had been really looking forward to welcoming them to our new home, and showing it in the best light. But as the day of their arrival drew closer, and the angle of the rain started to shift from vertical to horizontal (it was now coming in through the bottoms of the windows), excitement began to give way to anxiety.

On the morning of their arrival, I woke early and looked through the window to see blue skies. Maybe we were in luck, I thought, as I jumped out of bed and started to make plans for all kinds of wonderful trips and excursions. I was determined that this was going to be a visit to remember. But by mid-morning my plans were in disarray as the rain came pelting down again, even harder and heavier than before.

With most of the upper floor of the house still uncharted, we decided to accommodate the guests in the gîte. The layout was a bit strange. It turned out that Mrs Sumner's partner had been an architect and he seems to have tried out a few of his more eccentric ideas on the gîte. Basically, he transformed what was once a two-storey building into a five-storey building, without raising the roof. He did this by cleverly designing each floor as a split level, which meant you still really only had the same amount of floor area, but it was now divided up into separate spaces, which made it feel more open and free-flowing. It had also been done quite recently, so it was clean and modern and presentable. We switched on the electric heating the day before they arrived in order to have it nice and cosy, although, much like the main house, the gîte was also built of solid stone and did not retain the heat very well.

Despite our best efforts, the visit was a complete washout. We spent most of the week sitting in front of the fire, as it was too cold, wet and miserable to go outside. And anyway, there was nowhere to go, as everything seemed to be closed, probably until the tourist season began around Easter. It was really very disappointing. I wanted them to enjoy the visit and I suppose I also wanted them to be impressed; to see the property the same way we saw it on our first visit.

To make matters worse, the day before they were due to go home a plume of volcanic ash was blown into the sky somewhere over Iceland, bringing airline travel to a halt over most of northern Europe, including Ireland. With the realisation that they were to be confined to a cold, multi-storey gîte for at least another two days, I could see that Fiona was getting uneasy. On top of everything else, the late-night drinking and the lack of sober, restful sleep was now starting to get to all of us – we were tired, cold, grumpy and starting to feel a bit jittery around each other.

On day three of the ash problem, Fiona finally cracked: she attached herself to the computer and remained there until somehow she managed to find an alternative ash-free route home. It was expensive, and involved several changeovers, but they were determined, and I couldn't really blame them. They left early the next morning as the rain pummelled down from the skies and the Arctic temperatures almost reduced us to tears. As we waved goodbye, I had the fleeting thought that I wanted to go with them. I felt a lightness in my stomach, a longing for the safety and security of home.

We went back into the house to regroup. I lit the big open fire, Tanya made leek and potato soup and we all huddled up in front of the television to watch *Ratatouille*. By the time the film was over, we were already feeling better and looking forward again. I got up to open the curtains and, lo and behold, the sun had even made a welcome reappearance, and this time it felt hot. I went outside and, feeling slightly high at the prospect of better weather, I grabbed an old pair of hedge-cutters I found in the basement and started to attack overgrown bushes and shrubs that hadn't been touched for the best part of a decade, despite the fact that Mrs Sumner had been employing two so-called gardeners. It was exhilarating to be outdoors again, and to feel the warmth of the sun on my back as I set about revealing what lay beneath the overgrowth. It was a bigger job than I had anticipated, however, and before long I had traded the hedge-cutters for a handsaw, and not too long after that I realised that what I really needed was a chainsaw, which I did not have.

By lunchtime, I had cleared most of the thick scrub from around a second entrance to the property, revealing a beautiful old iron gate and an imposing pair of stone piers. This is what I love about old properties: the prospect of finding these little hidden treasures, of delving beneath the weeds or the dust or multiple layers of paint or paper and finding something old or ancient that opens a window to the past and fires up the imagination. Now all I had to do was to clean down the gate and give it a new coat of paint. But first I was ready for a hearty ploughman's lunch, and maybe even a short siesta. After all, we were supposed to be living the dream, as I had to keep reminding myself, and Tanya.

## The Disputed Territories

The siesta and the dream, the elusive dream, had to be put on hold once again, however, as shortly after lunch Lars arrived with some unsettling news. It seemed that while we had been distracted by other things, like the cold and the rain, our hostile agrarian neighbour had advanced on our northern flank. Lars informed me that a few days after my first encounter with Jacques he had erected a fence to separate his land from ours. It's a strange feature of the land in this area that there are often no fences and no clear boundaries between properties, and because Jacques had the use of our fields for so long, his land and ours had effectively become as one. Now, unfortunately, we had to grapple with the thorny issue of separating it again. Jacques had made the first move, but it seemed that his fence was well inside our boundary.

This was serious business, if it really was the case, but Lars warned us to be careful; land could be a very contentious issue. He told us a story about a land dispute between an English couple and a local farmer in a neighbouring commune, where the couple came home one day to find several bullet holes in a water tank in their garden. This was worrying but I told Lars that we weren't going to be bullied, which I think he appreciated. We drank a beer and talked it over and, for a while at least, it seemed like we had the situation under control.

Later, however, when Lars had gone home and the effects of the beer had worn off, bravado gave way to a slight nervousness. All this talk about guns and shooting into water tanks and the like was making me very uneasy. To make matters even worse, around this same time all the English news channels were reporting on an incident in the UK where a taxi driver had gone on a shooting rampage in a small village in Cumbria, killing twelve people. There had also just been an incident in Ireland, close to where I come from, where a young man, angered by the decision of his siblings to sell the family farm, had taken his legally held gun and shot dead the new owner. These stories weren't lost on me as I mulled over our own situation.

If we had been living in Ireland I probably would have been less concerned, as I found it easier there to weigh up a situation and the people involved, but in a small village in rural France, where I knew nothing about anybody, it was more difficult to get a handle on such things.

We needed to step back and take stock, and we also needed to get a proper map to see if we could work out the boundaries ourselves. We didn't want to make any accusations until we were absolutely sure he was in the wrong. He was still French after all, and a local, whereas we were just blow-ins and still unsure of our place in this new community. We secured the best map we could, and I examined it in great detail and then walked the land several times to see if I could identify the different points of reference. It didn't look like the fence was in the right place but I still wasn't sure. I checked the map again and, from what I could see, it looked like Jacques was occupying a small field that belonged to us.

The next morning, armed with my map and a mental assessment of the situation, I set off to see the mayor. He was in jovial mood, welcoming me to the commune and enquiring as to what plans we had for the property. I told him about some of our ideas for starting a gîte and B&B business and maybe even getting a few cattle and pigs. He seemed happy that we had all these great plans, and he was especially happy that we were planning to live there all year round, and send our children to the local school. This was a big deal in a commune where the average age was probably close to 70 and where the very survival of the local community, and its schools and other services, were always on a knife edge.

Eventually, I got around to the thorny subject of Jacques and the field and, as soon as I did, the mayor's mood changed instantly, from bubbly and chatty to cautious and withdrawn. In fairness, the French are not known for their ability to hide their emotions, and the mayor was no exception. It was obviously an issue he would have preferred not to have had to deal with, and he wasn't the only one. However, it seemed that he had already noticed the fence and he also had the impression that it was in the wrong place, but he didn't have too much faith in the map, which he said had only been produced for tax purposes and was not always accurate. He also said that these maps were old, and sometimes what appeared as a paddock on the map might have since reverted to woodland. Despite this, he still thought that the fence was in the wrong place, so he agreed to talk to Jacques. But he warned me that if Jacques didn't agree to move the fence, then my only option would be to get a surveyor, or *géomètre-expert*, as they are known in France, who would come and measure the land and then present a report, to be signed by both parties, which would be legally binding. This seemed like a good option, but it would be expensive and, as the instigators, we would have to pay.

A week later there was still no news from the mayor, so I set off to see him again. It was a nice sunny spring morning, so I decided to walk the few hundred metres to the village and, as I approached the *mairie* (mayor's office), I could see Jacques pushing a wheelbarrow full of cow dung along the street in front of his house. When he spotted me he wheeled off to the side of the street, just out of view, but out of the corner of my eye I could see him peering back around the corner, watching as I entered the *mairie*.

My meeting with the mayor didn't last long. He told me that he had spoken to Jacques, who insisted that he had put the fence in the right place and he wasn't prepared to move it. As the mayor saw it, we had two choices: let it lie, or get a *géomètre-expert*, at considerable expense to ourselves. He mentioned a figure of a couple of thousand euros. Clearly, he wanted us to let it lie, but as I saw it there was only one option: the *géomètre-expert*. If we rolled over now, God knows what liberties Jacques would take in the future. I told the mayor we were going for the nuclear option. He looked surprised, and I could tell he was mentally willing me to change my mind. I guess the prospect of an all-out feud between residents of this normally quiet and peaceful commune was not something he particularly relished. When he finally accepted what I was saying, he gave me the number of a *géomètre-expert* in Prayssac. He also, rather kindly, offered to come along on the day of the survey. I wasn't expecting this, but I appreciated the show of support.

I called the *géomètre-expert* later that day and, fortunately, his fee was in the hundreds rather than the thousands. We fixed a date for a meeting on-site the following week and he said he would notify Jacques, who would also have to be there. I phoned the mayor that evening to give him the news and I could hear the sense of dread and foreboding in his voice. I hung up feeling like Mister Pest. We were less than a month in the area and already we were tangled up in a messy dispute. It wasn't the start to our new life that I wanted, but it felt like we had no option.

I ambled into the living room, feeling tired and dejected. Tanya was there watching television; the kids were already in bed. I told her about my concern – that we were going to alienate ourselves and make an enemy of someone who had the potential to be dangerous. She had the same concern, but neither of us could see any alternative. We had to stand firm.

The following Wednesday morning, I set out for the front line and the 10.30 a.m. rendezvous with the *géomètre-expert*. The mayor was already there, standing near his car. The weather had turned bad again that morning and there were dark, heavy-looking clouds lingering overhead.

'There's going to be a storm', he said, prophetically. Seconds later, the heavens opened and we ran for cover in his car. While waiting for the others to arrive, we chatted about the unusually wet weather, our plans for Laborie, farming and sheep, and some other things I knew the French for. But behind my relatively calm exterior, I was decidedly uneasy and having serious second thoughts about the whole *géomètre-expert* thing. What kind of fools were we going to look if it turned out that Jacques was right? And this was a real possibility. Since my last meeting with the mayor I had checked the maps again and if, as he suggested, some paddocks had reverted to woodland, then that could change everything. Having brought things this far, there would be serious egg on our faces if we were wrong. I was on the verge of sharing my concerns with the major when the *géomètre-expert* and his assistant pulled in behind us. It was too late now, there was no turning back.

With the rain still pouring down, the *géomètre-expert*, Monsieur Rousseau, and his assistant, David, transferred from their car into the back seat of the mayor's. The mayor obviously knew them quite well and there was a friendly exchange; it seemed like everyone, bar me, was in pretty good spirits. A few minutes later Jacques arrived and, once the rain stopped, we all got out of our respective cars and shook hands. Jacques was friendly towards the *géomètre-expert* and his assistant and once the surveying started he launched a serious charm offence, the likes of which I didn't think he had in him – stories, jokes, laughter, there was no end to his repertoire. The mayor left after the initial introductions, and I remained pretty much in the background, my French not being really good enough to understand much of what was being said. After about two hours of measuring, walking, more measuring, checking under scrub for old boundary stones, head-scratching, and then more measuring, the results were finally in.

It was a big moment, and I guess there was always a risk in this kind of situation that someone might not be too pleased with the outcome, and could even blow a fuse, or maybe go completely berserk. People have fought and died over land and who was to say that this wouldn't be one of those occasions? But the *géomètre-expert* and his assistant were obviously aware of the dangers and they had a plan. This involved the *géomètre-expert* taking me in one direction, while his assistant took Jacques in another. As we walked, and as he explained to me how his measuring device worked and how accurate it was, he very casually informed me, almost by way of illustration, that Jacques had put his fence about two metres into our side of the field. The delivery was so matter-of-fact that the significance of it was completely lost on me. Was this a lot or very little? Was it just an innocent mistake or a deliberate land grab? Had we won or lost?

At the other side of the field, I was pretty sure Jacques was similarly perplexed. He stood in front of David with a bewildered look on his face and I could almost imagine what was going through his mind: was he being forced into a humiliating retreat? Or would it be just seen as window dressing to satisfy his cranky and oversensitive expat neighbour? But the more I thought about it, this was probably the best possible outcome, as it seemed like we were both winners, or, more accurately, neither of us was an outright loser.

The extent of the incursion was less than I had originally thought, but it was still two metres and, over a stretch of a few hundred metres, that wasn't insignificant. The *géomètre-expert* laid out some new boundary markers and explained to Jacques that he would have to move his fence. He didn't seem overly perturbed about this. He continued to laugh and joke with the *géomètre-expert*, which might have left me feeling suspicious had the mayor not vouched for the *géomètre-expert*'s credentials earlier.

To round off the proceedings, we all reconvened at the back of the *géomètre-expert*'s car, where we were asked to sign a map which showed the new boundary. Jacques signed, I signed, and that was it. Jacques then shook hands with the others, cracked another joke, probably about me, and off he went. The *géomètre-expert*'s assistant was going back to the field to take some final measurements so I walked with him and took the opportunity to ask his advice on how best to work out the rest of the boundary, much of which was also bordering land belonging to Jacques. Not surprisingly, the only possible solution he could think of was to hire a professional *géomètre-expert*, at great expense. I decided to postpone any decision on this for the time being. I had enough of land wars for a while and, anyway, I was keen to get on with living the life we had moved to France for, and it didn't involve *géomètre-expert*s. And so the frontier war was over. An anticlimax maybe, but I wasn't complaining about that. No one was dead or fatally wounded and the proper boundary had been identified and marked, and the treaty signed.

Nevertheless, the war had left its wounds: from then on Jacques and I never really spoke again. After a few months had passed I did begin to say *bonjour* if I met him on the road, but mostly he didn't respond. It was unfortunate. Looking back on it now, I think it was a genuine mistake on his part, but with no boundary markers, and maps that weren't fit for purpose, bringing in the *géomètre-expert* seemed like the only way to sort it out.

# 10

## The Cowboy Architect

With the frontier war behind us, we could finally refocus on more important matters, such as making a living, and getting our gîte and B&B business up and running before the summer. The gîte was in pretty good condition and basically just needed repainting and some new furniture. The B&B was a different story – the part of the house we planned to use for this needed complete renovation. There was also quite a bit of work to be done to get the pool and gardens into shape.

Like most people in our situation, in the early days we relied on a small network of local contacts, mainly expats, for information and advice. We soon discovered that this was a rather risky strategy, but in these first weeks we had no choice, as we had little else to go on. It was through this network that we got the name of a 'fantastic' local architect called Gregoire. From the glowing accounts we received, we had high hopes for Gregoire and we were really looking forward to meeting him and to getting his views on the renovations, so we phoned him and arranged for him to call to the house one Monday evening.

That weekend we talked through various plans and ideas, so by Monday we had a reasonably good idea of what we

wanted to do. We were ready and rearing to go. Five minutes before the agreed time of our meeting, we received a
phone call from Gregoire. He was very sorry but he had
been delayed at another meeting and he wanted to postpone
our appointment until Thursday. We were obviously disappointed, but we agreed to postpone.

On Thursday, just after lunch, a black sports car pulled
into the yard. I opened the front door and waited, expectantly, for the equally sporty occupant to leap from the car
and jog towards me. A minute or two later, the driver's door
opened and a black cowboy boot emerged, partly covered at
the top by a pair of sleek, black leather trousers. Maybe Jim
Morrison is not dead after all, I thought. But as the rest of
the trousers and a black suede jacket, topped off with a large
mop of frizzy grey-black hair, appeared, I realised that the
look was more Keith Richards than Jim Morrison.

'*Bonjour*, you must be Gregoire?', I enquired.

He said nothing as he stepped delicately towards the front
door, trying to avoid getting any mud on his boots. As he
came closer, I could see that he looked unsettled. The muddy
yard was obviously a problem, and he was also sniffling a
little and he looked pale and fragile. In fact, he looked like a
man who had been partying all night, and when he opened
his mouth, it sounded like someone had been rubbing sand-
paper on his larynx. Despite his delicate state, Gregoire was
our first real French guest (even though it was purely business) so I invited him into the kitchen to meet Tanya and to
have a cup of tea and a bit of a chat. As he shook hands with
Tanya, I could see her examining his necktie and silver cru-
cifix earrings, but he declined the cuppa and opted to stand
rather than sit.

He asked if we were English and, unusually for a French
person, he looked disappointed when we said we were Irish.
He said he loved the Beatles and Freddie Mercury. To try to
regain his interest, I told him that we had lived in Brussels
for many years and that we had just moved from there. He

seemed more interested in this, and then he told us that he had once designed a nightclub in Brussels. I'm not sure if he noticed our faces dropping at this point, but I was starting to feel a bit concerned about the idea of our new B&B being designed by an ageing rocker whose only experience that we knew of was designing a nightclub in Brussels. A disturbing vision of strip lighting and mirror balls was starting to form in my head.

The conversation pretty much ran to ground there, and it was obvious that Gregoire was in no mood for socialising. So, with the 'getting-to-know-each-other' session firmly knocked on the head, I guided him back out of the kitchen and into the right wing of the house, which we planned to use for the B&B. I started to explain some of our ideas to Gregoire, but I quickly got the sense that I was boring him. He stared at me blankly as I rabbited on about traditional stone floors and rustic charm. At first I put it down to my poor French, but as the one-sided conversation wore on I realised that he just didn't give a feck. After about ten minutes, I was actually getting bored listening to myself, so I asked him if he had enough information to prepare some plans (knowing full well that we hadn't covered a fraction of what he needed to know). He said he did and that he would be in touch again soon. I wondered to myself if that meant with me or with mankind in general, but before I could say, 'You haven't taken any measurements yet', the black cowboy was hauling himself back into the black Megane and riding off into the sunset.

A few days went by and we heard nothing from Gregoire. After a week, I phoned him to see if the plans were ready, but he said he needed to come by to take some more measurements. A few days later, he arrived again. Dressed in a similar outfit, he seemed just a tad more sociable this time. He also looked less sickly. He took the necessary measurements and said he would send us the plans by e-mail before the end of the week. He would also prepare estimates for the work and then get the workmen to come by and give more exact quotes. True to his word, the plans came by the end of the week, with the estimates, which seemed reasonable. A few days after that, the workmen – a plumber/electrician (these two professions go together in France), a tiler and a painter – had all been in and the quotes were starting to arrive. Amazingly, there were no major surprises; all the prices were within our expectations and everybody seemed keen to get on with the job.

Having agreed to all the quotes, including Gregoire's commission for the plans and project management, a date was set to start the work. We were close, so tantalisingly close to something going smoothly that I had a feeling it was almost too good to be true. Sure enough, the day before the official start date, Gregoire phoned with some bad news. His team of workers was very busy and he asked if we would mind postponing everything for a week. We had no real problem with this – a week didn't sound so unreasonable. Then, a week later, Gregoire phoned again. His electrician/plumber had just too much work on and he wanted to know if we would be able to find someone else. This was a more serious problem, as basically we knew nobody in the area, especially no electrician/plumbers, and this was also probably the biggest part of the work, but it felt like we had no choice, so we took it on the chin. Later that day, Gregoire phoned again, this time to inform us that the rest of the team were still busy and would not be able to start for another week.

The following night, around 9 p.m., he arrived with the tiler, to have another look at what needed to be done. We went through everything in great detail again and then the tiler announced that he would only be able to do the bathroom, but not the floors in the other rooms. He was just too busy and his wife was stuck in Reunion and couldn't get back because of a strike. We weren't sure what bearing the latter had on his decision but the bottom line was that we would also need to find another tiler. First it was the plumber/

electrician, and now the tiler – I told Gregoire to forget it, that we would manage the project ourselves. If we had to get another tiler for the other rooms then he might as well just do everything. Gregoire apologised and seemed genuinely sorry, but he had no other advice to offer; we were on our own. When they left, I turned to Tanya and threw my hands up in the air like a true Frenchman.

To add insult to injury, the next morning Gregoire was back again, knocking on the door at 9 a.m., looking more sprightly this time. At first I thought he might have come back to tell us that he had found a couple of very handy tradesmen who were ready to start work immediately, so when he presented me instead with a bill for drawing up the plans, I was a bit surprised. I examined the bill on the spot and was shocked to find that he was looking for €500. It seemed steep, and I felt compelled to remind him of our agreement: that he would get a percentage of the overall price for the job, as long as it was completed to our satisfaction. Gregoire had little interest in discussing agreements, however, and rather than stay arguing with him all day long, I paid him the €500, and put it down to an expensive first lesson in the peculiarities of doing business in a foreign country.

Later that morning, I phoned Catherine, one of our English neighbours, who had recommended a guy called Pierre who had just done some work on her house. Catherine gave me Pierre's phone number and I phoned him straight away. He sounded nice enough; we discussed the work and he said he would drop by the following Saturday to see what needed doing.

§

In the meantime, the bad weather continued. In fact, it was now officially the coldest and wettest April on record. We had the central heating on, and switched to the highest setting, but in a big old house with stone walls and 5 millimetre gaps around the windows it was a bit like trying to fill a basket with water. So, as we waited for workmen and warmer weather to arrive, I retreated to my small office in the tower, where I clung on to an electric heater and tried to get some work done and bring in some money.

It was still early days, but the thought did cross my mind, more than once, that we had just voluntarily moved from a cosy, well-insulated, townhouse in the trendy east district of Brussels to a draughty, impossible-to-heat stone house in the extremities of rural France. For some reason, however, and it was certainly nothing obvious or logical, it still seemed like the right decision. Maybe it was the anticipation of better things to come, or a romantic attachment to the life we were trying to create rather than the one we were actually living. If so, then maybe there was some reprieve on the horizon.

## The Hunters' Ball

The day of the hunters' ball finally arrived and we were very excited about the prospect of meeting the locals and participating in our first event as residents of a rural French village. Dressed up in our best garb, we set off for the village at about 11.45 a.m. On the way we dropped in for Lars and Helena and, together, all six of us walked the 300 metres or so to the village, basking in beautiful spring sunshine. As we approached the centre of the village, I could see there were a lot of people standing around in front of the *foyer rurale*, which is a kind of community hall found in nearly all rural villages in France. In our village, the *foyer rurale* was housed in an old wine cellar, with a beautiful vaulted ceiling. This was one of many remnants of a time, before the devastating phylloxera disease, and before the big frost of 1957, when the village was surrounded by vineyards. Now there was only one small vineyard left in the commune, with most of the area's wine production confined to a smaller but expanding area in the direct vicinity of the River Lot.

We moved through the small crowd, not really knowing anyone, even though Lars and Helena did shake a few hands and nod in a few directions. Inside the *foyer rurale*, preparations were well under way: there was a bar at one end, at the back of which was a kitchen, where I could see five or six elderly women buzzing about with pots and pans. Anne, a local woman, was behind the bar, pouring some kind of aperitif into plastic glasses. We had gotten to know Anne quite well as she was looking after Astrid a few days a week. She lived in the centre of the village and, unlike many of the locals, she was young – well, late thirties or early forties. She was also very friendly, but she spoke so quickly and with such a strong accent that it was difficult to understand her sometimes.

Behind the bar, Anne was being ably assisted by two men from the village, who were part of a group of five or six men who were involved in just about everything that went on in the commune. We later discovered that the reason for this was because they were elected members of the mayor's advisory committee – the *conseil municipal*. Between the three of them, they were struggling to cater for the thirsty villagers, who were now three deep at the bar. But, despite the brisk trade, as soon as she caught sight of us, Anne immediately downed tools and raced out to greet us in customary fashion, bestowing multiple kisses on all of our cheeks. She was quite animated and speaking at her usual 100 miles per hour, so I only managed to grasp one bit of what she said, which was that she had reserved seats for us at her table. This was very kind of her and it was nice to be made feel welcome. Having imparted this crucial information, she reached across the bodies huddled around the bar and grabbed some drinks for us. We made our way to our assigned table, where Lars and Helena were also seated, as well as a local English couple. It felt reassuring to be around people we already knew, and people who spoke English, but it was also nice to be in the company of some local French people.

The cellar was long, at least 25 or 30 metres, and the tables were laid out crossways in two rows, leaving a long aisle down the middle of the room. There were about twelve people per table, six either side, and each table had been pre-set with jugs of red wine and baskets of bread. Energised by the punchy aperitifs, the tables were soon buzzing with conversation and laughter. Our little multinational group toasted our mutual good health several times, once in each language, including Irish, and, as soon as the aperitifs were gone, we followed the example of the neighbouring tables and tucked into the jugs of red wine.

With all the drinking and friendly banter, it felt almost like home. The difference, however, as I would notice later in the day, was that nobody would get inebriated. It was all very civilised and convivial and people just instinctively knew where to draw the line. What a relief it was to know that we could bring our children up in this kind of environment, where people could enjoy the pleasures of drinking without going too far.

Before we had a chance to get too giddy on the wine, several big plates of venison and wild boar meat landed on our table, just in time to temper the mood and maintain us on an even keel for the remainder of the afternoon. It was a wonderful occasion and what was particularly notable was the feeling of timelessness. The ancient building, the local wine, meat from the surrounding woods, vegetables from the village gardens – it was probably how it had been for centuries, and that made it all the more special.

A good three hours later, just as the desserts were arriving, the president of the hunters' association took to his feet to welcome everyone and to recount a few highlights of another good year for the hunters. He then invited the mayor to address the gathering. The mayor told a funny story. The reason I know this is because the French-speaking people sitting around me threw their heads back in laughter at various intervals. Personally, I hardly understood a word of what he said. I was still struggling with the local accent.

Towards the end of his speech, I understood more of what he was saying, mainly because he was talking about us. From his standing position, he moved towards our table and, in his most eloquent French, he warmly welcomed us to the commune and expressed his delight that we had chosen this area to bring up our young children. He wished us a very long and happy life at Laborie, which he described as the most beautiful house in the commune, and somewhere the entire community was very happy to hear the sound of children again. It was completely unexpected but we were really delighted to receive such a public welcome from the mayor, and after everything that had happened with Jacques the farmer, this really helped us to feel part of the community.

We also met some really nice people that day, French and English, some of whom would soon become good friends. One of these was Jean-Luc, a single man in his late fifties or early sixties who lived alone in a little house just outside the village. Jean-Luc's family had lived in the area for generations and he was well known as a great source of information on all things to do with the locality and its history. Since we had moved to the area, I had been trying, with little success, to find out about the history of Laborie, so I was delighted when he promised to drop by and tell me all he knew. He also told me that there were truffiers (trees under which truffles grew) on our land and that he would bring his dog, Biscuit, who was trained in the dark art of truffle hunting. Foolishly, I somehow assumed that this would be some day the following week, but as the days and weeks went by I began to think that Jean-Luc had forgotten about our little engagement. Now and then I would see him passing by on the road in his ageing Renault van, with five or six dogs leaping around inside, like clothes in a tumble drier, while Jean-Luc focused intently on the road ahead, oblivious to the circus going on around him.

Then, about three months after the hunters' ball, when I had almost forgotten about our arrangement, he drove into the yard one day and nonchalantly suggested that we take Biscuit for a walk in the woods and have a chat about local history. We set off together down the field and into the woods and, while Biscuit sniffed his way from one potential truffier to the next, Jean-Luc told me everything he knew about Laborie. He started by emphasising that Laborie was considered to be the finest house in the commune (therefore, it was known locally as 'le château') and the locals were very proud of it. It wasn't actually a château in the sense of being a castle or large manor house, but in the context of the village and the surroundings it was important. The property had once been a vineyard, but that probably ceased in the second half of the nineteenth century with the outbreak of phylloxera. Since then, the more fertile and workable land had been converted to pasture, while the stonier and steeper areas were effectively abandoned. These abandoned areas, over time, naturally regenerated as oak, chestnut and beech forests, which now covered about half of the property and most of the commune, and department.

Jean-Luc told me that, as a child, he remembered passing by the gates of the house on his way to school in the village. At that time, the property was owned by two sisters, who were always dressed in black, the traditional clothing of the time, and one of them was fond of the drink. In fact, the young Jean-Luc and his buddies were scared for their lives of the two women, who were elderly at this stage, and he told me how they would run past the gate for fear one of the old women might catch them. When the sisters died, the property was bought by a doctor from Cahors and after that by a wealthy businessman who, according to Jean-Luc, made the house available for other wealthy friends from the Cahors area to bring their mistresses. I could see now why the locals were happy to see children there once again. It wasn't quite the historical account I was expecting, at least not the latter part, and if there were truffles on our property, they certainly weren't making themselves known to Biscuit, so all in all it wasn't the bountiful expedition I had hoped for, but it was a pleasant couple of hours nonetheless.

## Our First Booking ... Almost!

The income from the gîte and B&B was going to be important for our financial security and we hadn't wasted any time in trying to get it up and running. During our first week, we took some nice photos of the gîte, prepared a little blurb and then posted an advertisement on four different websites. With everything else that was going on, we then forget about it for a few weeks until one day, out of the blue, Tanya received an e-mail enquiry. It was a Sunday morning; the kids were playing in the living room and Tanya and I were sitting in the kitchen, drinking tea and reading the Irish newspapers on our laptops. It was a rare but welcome moment of peace and tranquility, which was suddenly turned on its head by the antics of a hyper-animated woman dancing around the kitchen floor, shouting:

'We've got our first booking, we've got a booking, we've got a booking!'

Having been immersed in news stories of dodgy property developers and struggling mortgage holders, I had no idea what was going on at first, but I was amused to see my wife in such high spirits. Then my distracted brain caught up, and I remembered something about us having accommodation for rent. I jumped to my feet and joined Tanya in the celebrations. Hearing the commotion, Ned and Astrid also joined in, and we all danced and hugged in the middle of the kitchen floor.

'And it's for one month!', Tanya shouted excitedly.

Hearing that, my heart sank. I tried to hide any look of disappointment, as I didn't want to spoil the moment, but I just knew something wasn't right. Nobody books a gîte for a month.

'What's wrong?', Tanya enquired, sensing that my appetite for wild celebration had suddenly waned.

'Nothing!', I assured her, but when things calmed down a little and the kids had gone back to the living room, I asked her for a few more details.

'It's from a guy called Dr David Francis', she said. 'Do you think that name sounds a bit weird?'

Weird, maybe. But certainly not as weird as the fact that he wanted to pay everything up front by cheque, including spending money, which we were supposed to keep for him after we had cashed the cheque. It was, of course, a scam, and the following morning we reported it to the company that owned the website, who then sent a warning to other non-suspecting advertisers. It wouldn't be the last such message we received, but we were a little bit wiser from then on.

Things went quiet for another few days after that and we were starting to wonder if we were ever going to get a real booking. Then, about a week later, some genuine enquiries started to come in, and on 21 April we got our first booking – for one week in August. The following day, another week in August was booked, and then a friend from Ireland booked the B&B for ten days in July. From then on, we had a steady stream of enquiries and bookings and we began to feel more confident about the package we had on offer. The swimming pool was clearly a big selling point; in fact it was the first question on most people's list, and I suspect that if we didn't have one we would have struggled. With the bookings progressing well, we urgently needed to start the renovations on the B&B and to knock the gardens and swimming pool into shape. With the search for alternative builders already in train, I decided to focus my attention on the gardens.

For some reason, we had given absolutely no consideration to how we were going to look after the gardens and grounds before we bought the house. I think we just assumed they would look after themselves, or that it wouldn't be very onerous. Boy did we get that wrong – spectacularly wrong! Our first *bête noire* was the grass. By the end of April, it had grown a foot high and I was starting to get concerned that it might have gone beyond the scope of a lawnmower. I knew we had to do something, quickly, and, with over two acres of lawns, a sit-on lawnmower seemed like the only option, so I started to draw up a shopping list. Beyond the vast open spaces of lawn, there was also a myriad of smaller spaces and steep slopes that no ride-on lawnmower could access. For such elusive patches of earth, a strimmer was needed, so this was item number two on my list. The next must-have tool was a chainsaw. No self-respecting country bumpkin has a tool shed without a chainsaw taking pride of place, and for very good reason. As well as the obvious rite-of-passage benefits, it was also a central part of our master plan for eco-living and the exploitation of our 20-odd acres of woodland.

To maintain all this heavy-duty machinery, we were also going to need a proper tool kit, multiple jerry cans and, to avoid losing some vital body parts, a few pieces of protective gear. The total bill came to just over €2,000, which also included a garden trailer for the ride-on lawnmower. It was an expense we hadn't bargained for, but in the absence of going back to Iron Age practices of cutting grass with a scythe and chopping down trees with an axe, there was really no other way.

## Renaissance Man

It is said that necessity is the mother of invention, and nowhere is this truer than in the depths of the French countryside, where the nearest shops are a good twenty minutes' drive away, and it's almost impossible to find 'professional' handymen to do any kind of small odd jobs. Instead, people rely on their own resourcefulness to take care of those blocked pipes or leaky roofs, and it's decidedly uncool, in a country sense, if you didn't know how. I never really considered myself handy when it came to this kind of thing, probably because I lived in a city for most of my adult life, where a man with a spanner or a toolbox was never more than a phone call away, but now I found myself in the firing line and forced to have a go. Strangely enough, I found myself half-enjoying these little challenges and I was surprised by the fact that I actually turned out to be, dare I say it, kind of handy. On top of this, I discovered that it was quite liberating and empowering not to be dependent on someone else to fix the kids' toys, mend a leaky toilet or jump-start the car. The best thing of all, though, was that by learning to fix and mend things we cut down considerably on the amount of waste we produced, and while this kind of frugality arose by necessity rather than being part of any great master plan, it soon became a very important means of saving money and of being more eco-friendly, which was also something we felt strongly about.

As time went on, my newfound manifestation of handiness also extended to the fixing and servicing of garden tools and equipment, but to my great regret now, there was still one activity that I didn't really have the time to tackle – building! Therefore, having watched our French cowboy architect ride off into the night, we were forced to resume our search. I had already made an appointment with a French builder called Pierre, and next on the list was an Englishman who had been suggested by a local English couple we met at the hunters' ball. They didn't have any first-hand experience of his work, but he had done some work for some friends of theirs who lived nearby. We were quite excited about the prospect of finding a capable builder, so the day after the ball, on our way to the supermarket in Prayssac, we drove past their house to see if there was anyone home. I rang the doorbell and I could hear a woman's voice calling inside, but it took several minutes before the door finally opened. A grey-haired woman in her mid-fifties emerged and stood looking at me very sternly without uttering a word. I felt I needed to explain myself, and quickly.

'Hello, I'm looking for Jan Peeters; I hope I've got the right house?', I enquired, assuming she understood English.

'JAAAAAN', she bellowed in the direction of the stairs, before turning and disappearing again without uttering a word to me. A few minutes later, Jan appeared. He was a smallish, fit-looking man, with lightly tanned skin and short, neatly trimmed grey hair. He was about fifty, well groomed and with the look of someone who was not short of money. He seemed friendly. I explained why we had dropped by and he immediately insisted on giving us a tour of the house, to see what the builder had done. It was really well finished, and Jan told us that a guy called Dave had done all the work. I asked him if it would be possible to get Dave's phone number but Jan went one step further – he offered to bring Dave to see us the following afternoon.

Around 3 p.m. the following day, Jan and Dave arrived in Jan's silver Mercedes. I showed them around the house and barn and then we settled down on the terrace for a cold beer and a chat. Jan was just as friendly as he had been the day before, and even more talkative. Dave was a different character altogether: much quieter and slightly shifty looking. He was younger than Jan, probably mid-forties, and more rugged looking, with a shaven head, faded jeans and a loose hanging white vest. As it was Sunday and the weather was nice, we didn't get into the nitty gritty of the work. Instead, we arranged for Dave to come back the following day to talk through it in more detail. The next day, Dave arrived as agreed and, like any good builder, his very first act was to pit husband against wife by suggesting a variety of elaborate but expensive changes to our original plans, such as a bigger bathroom.

I had found Dave a bit aloof the day before, but he was more talkative without Jan around, which wasn't necessarily such a good thing. He delivered the quote the following

Friday, a day late, but I guessed that probably stood up well in comparison to the industry average. It was about what we expected – not cheap, but not over the top either, and even though I had some reservations about Dave himself, I was reassured by what we had seen at Jan's house. He said he would phone on Saturday evening to discuss the quote, but when he phoned he instead invited us to call around to his house the following day, to see the work he had done there. The house was just outside Cahors; it was a converted barn, and, as Dave had done the conversion himself, it seemed to be his showpiece. It did look good, with a very impressive living area that used the full height of the barn, with exposed beams and stonework. Dave suggested that he would show us the rest of the house, but we already liked what we saw so I told him that we were happy with the quote and that if he still wanted it, he had the job. I was hoping this would avoid the need for a hard sell, but it seemed that Dave had already prepared his pitch, so we still had to go through the motions.

It was a relief to have finally found a builder and to know that the work could now proceed on the B&B. At least that was the plan, but life is never that simple and, within seconds of leaving Dave's house, just as we pulled away in the car, Tanya casually launched a hand grenade in my direction:

'Did I tell you that Lars met Dave somewhere recently and he was reeking of alcohol and having a major barney with his wife?'

'He must have just had a few too many', I said, trying not to get too alarmed.

'Yes, but it was in the middle of the day, and Lars thinks Dave has a drink problem. He said there was something about the look in his eye; he'd seen it before in other guys he knew had problems with drugs and alcohol.'

'Really, that's interesting, but why didn't you mention this earlier, before we actually hired him to come and work in our house?'

'Well, I would have had but Lars told me not to tell you.'

This was too much to get my head around, so I decided to just block it out in the hope that it was all a big mistake. Dave called the following Tuesday to say he would be on-site by the end of the week.

# 11

## Living the Green Dream

It was a balmy Saturday evening towards the end of April when a nice man from a certain renewable energy company dropped by. I had met his colleague at an exposition in Puy-l'Évêque a couple of weeks earlier and arranged for an on-site assessment of our renewable energy production potential. Our hope was that we would eventually be able to produce all our own heat and electricity on site, and maybe even sell a surplus back to the grid, but it was a complex area. There were a lot of new systems and technologies on the market so we needed some professional advice.

The man parked his car on the road and walked up the lane to the house. At first he seemed a bit uneasy or maybe unsure of himself, but once we got chatting he seemed to relax. We spoke about the house, the village, sport, Ireland and many other things and he was quite friendly, albeit still a little nervous. We chatted for quite a while, until it felt like we had exhausted every possible line of conversation, but he was still in no rush to talk business, despite the fact that it was getting late on Saturday evening. So it was left to me to steer the conversation in that direction. I explained that we were interested in looking at the possibility of generating electricity using solar (PV) panels. I showed him where I thought we could put the panels and then he set about taking some measurements. Strangely, however, the measuring didn't stop there, as once that was done he continued to measure other parts of the property: the perimeter of the house, the garden wall, the lawn, and just about everything else that was amenable to being measured.

After a couple of hours of this, I started to think he was just measuring for fun, that it was some kind of hobby, or even an obsession, but I later discovered that this is typical of French tradesmen – they just love to measure things. But what made Mr Renewables stand out was the fact that he didn't use a measuring device. Instead, he was relying solely on the good old 'step-it-out' approach. He wasn't a big man either, no more than 5'5" or 5'6", so his footsteps weren't the longest, and he sometimes started from roughly somewhere in the middle of the distance he was measuring and then doubled up.

With the entire property measured, we retired to the house for some refreshments. I asked him if he would like some tea or coffee and he opted for tea, with a devious-looking grin on his face. Tanya put a cup in front of him and he stared at it in the same way he had stared at me all evening – a mixture of bemusement and bewilderment.

'Do I put sugar in it?'

I told him that he could if he liked it sweet, but not everyone did. He thought about this for a minute and then announced that he would put sugar in it because, from what he understood, that was what you were supposed to do. It was around 7.30 p.m. at this stage, which was past feeding time for the children, both of whom were tired and hungry after a long day outdoors, so as Mr Renewables savoured his exotic tea experience, chaos erupted all around him. Astrid screamed at the top of her voice, insisting that she just had to sit on my knee, while Ned followed Tanya around the kitchen, pulling on her leg and repeatedly asking for biscuits. I felt sorry for the poor man, but he was too busy staring into his tea cup to really notice what was going on.

He was old school, and a likeable character, but sadly the prices he later quoted us were just too high. We also got quotes from several other companies and it was the same thing. It just wasn't a feasible proposition. This was disappointing. Part of the dream was to live a greener life, and to be as self-sufficient as possible in order to keep our costs to a minimum, but the economics of it just didn't stack up. To make the entire project work, we had to invest our money wisely and green investment and smart investment were proving difficult to reconcile.

## The Hidden Costs

One aspect of life in France that I had been really looking forward to was being able to just walk out the door and straight into nature, into our own fields and woods. In the first weeks, I did manage to take advantage of this most days but, as with many other aspects of our new life, I soon realised that such pleasures came at a price. On my regular stroll around the fields I started to notice how unchecked scrub was encroaching from the woods and hedgerows, not only reducing the area of useable land but also giving the fields a dirty, uncared-for appearance. A couple of trees had also fallen into the fields and most of the stone walls that existed were badly damaged, mainly due to the relentless passage of wild animals.

The countryside can be very beautiful, but when part of it belongs to you, you start to look at it differently. Whereas previously I might have considered such imperfections as a normal feature of the landscape, I now saw them as something that needed dealing with – a responsibility. I wanted the property to look like it was cared for and I was discovering that that wasn't going to happen by itself. After one of my regular morning walks, I got a tad impatient and decided I was going to take action forthwith. It was still early, about

8 a.m., but I headed straight for the garage, where I started up our new ride-on lawnmower and set off, determinedly, for a particularly unsightly patch of scrub in a field at the rear of the house. Within a matter of seconds I had three flat tyres and was forced to abandon my hare-brained plan. The scrub was incredibly pernicious, with long, rigid thorns that went straight through the tyres of the lawnmower. With my tool of choice now out of action, I did what any grown-up country man with the bit between his teeth would do – I grabbed a stick from the wood and started to swing wildly at the spikey culprits. I managed to take a few casualties, and to release some pent-up aggression, but I eventually realised that this kind of psychotic behaviour was not the way to deal with encroaching scrub. I retreated to the safety of the house for some much-needed reflection.

The next morning I got up feeling refreshed, recharged and ready to take on challenges anew. On the basis of the previous day's experience, I had excluded the idea of taking on the scrub again, at least until I had acquired a more effective tool than a stick. Instead, my target on this fine morning was another once alluring feature of the property, the maintenance of which we had also completely overlooked, or at least underestimated – the swimming pool. We had opened it up for the season a few days previously, but it now needed to be cleaned and treated on a daily basis in order to keep the green algae at bay.

At this point, I knew absolutely nothing about the maintenance of swimming pools. When we bought the house, we only saw the romantic side of it – stretching out on our inflatables on those hot summer days, sipping something mildly alcoholic and contemplating the finer things in life. Fishing out dead rabbits, snakes, mice, frogs, insects and endless amounts of leaves and other debris never even crossed our minds. Nor did the daily sessions with a giant vacuum cleaner, or the cleaning of the skimmers or back-washing the sand filter, or even the regular water sampling and tinkering around with test tubes to measure pH and chlorine levels. But this, I discovered, was the reality of having a pool, and during our first summer in France I spent at least an hour every morning from May until October on pool maintenance. It was an eye opener, and you probably could have counted on one hand the amount of times I actually swam in the damn thing.

Then there was the garden, all two acres of it, which again sounded great in theory, and would be a great space to enjoy, if it was someone else's. But when it's yours you see another side to it. You see how unwilling nature is to conform to man's attempts to impose order and structure. You see the relentless growth of the grass, the waywardness of the hedges, the unruliness of the nettles, and the seemingly endless desire all round for growth and invasion. Cutting the grass was a weekly chore from about the end of March onwards, and it required almost a half-day to get it all done. The weeding, hedge-trimming, strimming and other tasks required another few hours every week – and then there was the vegetable garden. Growing our own organic fruit and vegetables was another part of our plan for the dream life. We were fortunate in that the garden was already endowed with lots of mature fruit trees: apple, pear, mirabelle, plum and cherry, but there was no vegetable plot, so this we had to develop. We started digging in early April, turning over sods that hadn't been turned for decades, or maybe never. The soil was heavy, sticky and knitted together with a dense network of roots. It was back-breaking work, but we eventually dug and cleared a patch of about ten square metres, which we conditioned with lots of compost. At the end of April, a little later than ideal, we busily set about planting tomatoes, lettuces, onions, potatoes, beetroot, aubergines, courgettes, basil, parsley and just about anything else we could think of. It was exciting, and the anticipation of a bountiful harvest had our mouths watering. The less exciting bit was the twenty weeks of weeding and watering that came between the planting and the harvesting. The warm, dry climate meant there was a near daily requirement for watering, especially during July and August, and with the heat and plenty of water came some fairly spectacular growth, of the good and the bad. Once we stripped away the weeds, however, our hard work was duly rewarded with some of the nicest vegetables I have ever tasted. The tomatoes were spectacularly good, as were the aubergines, which thrived in the warm climate. In general, we had more than we could eat. This also applied to the fruit; so much of what we harvested was converted into jams and chutneys to be enjoyed throughout the year.

I must admit, I did like the outdoor work, and it was a welcome change from sitting in front of a computer all day, but I hadn't bargained on so much of it, and as we headed towards the summer, I was looking at about the equivalent of two days per week on outdoor maintenance work, which was pretty comfortably going to absorb any free time I hoped to have. It was also becoming clear to me that I would have to take some kind of French course, and then there was the oil-painting course I signed up for, which would be another half-day per week. And somewhere in between all of this I also planned to spend more time with my family, and hold down a day job. Moving to France might have changed the rules of engagement, but the old enemy was still the same – time. Something was going to have to give.

Tanya was faring better on this front. She had busy periods, especially on Saturdays, which was the change-over day for the gîte, but otherwise she seemed to be able to find more time to enjoy life. A bigger issue for her, however, was the fact that she didn't have someone to enjoy it with, as I seemed to be busy with something else most of the time, and when I was around, I was probably stressed and not very good company.

## Identified Flying Objects

Another dark secret lurking in the beautiful outdoors was the insects, yet another addition to the growing list of things we hadn't considered before the move. The first plague of insects to descend on us was the ants, giant ants. It happened out of the blue. We woke up one morning and there were literally thousands of them – in the house, outside the house, by the pool, in the gardens, everywhere, and, having no prior experience in ant extermination, we were totally unprepared. My first rather naïve response was to pour boiling water into the nests, but this was nothing more than a hot shower for them. They thrived on it. Then Lars suggested some kind of insecticide powder, which you scatter along their marching route. But they simply changed route and continued to scurry back and forth, hauling pieces of food that were double or treble their own body weight. The best solution, which we only discovered after weeks of messing around with all kinds of other useless potions and concoctions, was a little plastic disc that contained an insecticide in gel form. The ants were attracted into the disc by the scent of the gel, which they fed on, and probably lathered themselves in, and then brought it back to the nests where it wiped out the entire population. Voila! It was clean, safe and very effective.

We eventually got the ants under control, but there was no time to rest on our laurels as sometime in early May the mosquitoes arrived. For some people, mosquitoes don't seem to be a major problem. They never seem to go near Tanya, for example. For years I was convinced she must have had some kind of inbuilt repellent, and then I discovered that her inbuilt repellent was in fact me – as long as I was around, the mosquitoes only ever seemed to have eyes for me. Tanya didn't exist. Luckily it's the same for the kids, who have obviously inherited Tanya's mosquito-repelling genes. On the other hand, they love me, especially female mosquitoes – the ones that bite. They look at me and see chocolate cake with a big dollop of double cream on top, while other people in my company look like Brussels sprouts. If I was a young male mosquito this might be a cause for celebration, but as a not-so-young man, it is hell on earth. As their numbers grew,

I just couldn't go outdoors after 6 p.m., and if I did I had to be dressed in such a way that literally only the whites of my eyes were showing, which is not much fun when it's 35 degrees Celsius. In fact, even when I was covered head to toe they still seemed to be able to find some means of penetration, and there always seemed to be two or three of them waiting for me in the bedroom at night.

The low point came one evening when we returned from a very tiring and stressful trip to Ikea in Toulouse. It was about 7 p.m. on a hot, sticky evening in early June when we finally pulled into the front yard. By this stage, I really just wanted to crash out in front of the television with a beer. I was physically and mentally exhausted. But as we had to return the rented van we were using early the following morning, everything had to be unloaded straight away. Reluctantly, I dragged myself from the van and started to haul out the first of many flat packs. It was still well over 30 degrees and even though I was dressed down to shorts and a light T-shirt, within minutes I was in a lather of sweat – or, to the mosquitoes, a lather of highly alluring perfume. It didn't take long, therefore, before the love-fest began. At first it was my legs, but this was a regular occurrence by now, so I soldiered on without taking too much notice. A short while later, I could feel the biting on my arms, under my armpits and even on my ears, which was a first.

At this point, the combination of fatigue, stress, heat and multiple toxic injections was really starting to take its toll. But the van just had to be emptied and returned the following morning and there was nobody else to do it, so I doused myself in lemon juice and charged over the top once again. About halfway through the job, having dropped the last piece of the *Svelvik* in the bedroom, I was making my way back to the van when I noticed a dark cloud overhead. It was a warm, hazy evening so at first I didn't take too much notice, putting it down to humidity, but as I got closer I could see that this particular cloud had nothing to do with humidity – this was a living, breathing cloud, made up of millions or even billions of very excited mosquitoes. It actually covered the entire front of the house but was at its most dense around the van. The sensible thing to do at this stage would have been to double back and take refuge in the safety of the house. The insane thing to do, especially if you were known to be an object of erotic desire to mosquitoes, would have been to wander half-naked and sweaty into the middle of the cloud – and this is why I think I must have been suffering from mental exhaustion.

Without any care for my own welfare, or the welfare of those who depended on me, I marched onward into the eye of the storm. Within seconds I was on the wrong end of possibly one of the greatest trouncings ever given to a man by hyper-aroused insects. The biting was relentless and excruciating. I lurched forwards, then backwards, not really sure where I was going, and unable to see clearly due to the pain and the shear density of insects in the air around me. I eventually made it to the van and crawled in backwards, kicking at a *Skoghall* bedside table that was holding the left door open. As I was doing this, I noticed my legs and arms had changed colour. I panicked and kicked the doors closed, realising almost immediately that I had made a terrible mistake: I had just locked myself in, and by this stage there were almost as many mosquitoes in the van as outside. Realising the gravity of the situation, I pushed the *Skoghall* to one side and leaped towards the back of the van, frantically searching in the half-light for an inside latch, but there was nothing; the bloody thing could not be opened from the inside. This was not how my life was supposed to end – trapped in the back of a Fiat Ducato with an army of overexcited mosquitoes.

I yelled out for Tanya but got no response. I screamed at the top of my voice, but still not a dicky bird. I was hyperventilating at this stage and not thinking straight, so I sat down in the van and took a couple of deep breaths, which unfortunately resulted in the inhalation of half a dozen of the little buggers. As I sat there contemplating my next move, the humming grew louder and louder and the van started to feel hotter and hotter and smaller and smaller.

Compose yourself, they're only little insects, I told myself, trying to avert further panic.

But what if I have so many bites that I experience some kind of toxic shock. I could be dead in minutes … 'TANYAAAA!!'

'What's wrong?', came a voice from the distance.

'I'm stuck, the door won't open and I'm being eaten by mozzies. Can you get me out of here?'

A minute or two later the doors swung open and I leaped out and ran to the house. Inside, Tanya applied several different kinds of creams and lotions, as I struggled to stave off the onset of post-traumatic stress disorder. This was the worst encounter I ever had with mosquitoes, before or since, and it left its marks. The good news, however, is that we still managed to get the van back the next morning.

In the weeks that followed, the battle with the mosquitoes continued, albeit at a lower intensity, and it was only towards the end of the summer that it finally dawned on us that maybe there was a connection between the unusually large numbers of mosquitoes and the stagnant pond of water at the side of the house. With our new trusted adviser on all things French and beyond, our neighbour Marcel, I set about syphoning the water from the pond, letting it run off down the field. It took a couple of days to drain completely but the effect was immediate: in less than a week the mosquitoes had all but disappeared.

A few weeks later, I even had the bare-faced cheek to sit on the terrace in a shorts and T-shirt one evening. Admittedly, it was a bit provocative, and maybe I was asking for it, but, to my great relief, it seemed that the mosquitoes had indeed moved on to pastures new.

§

With the ants and mosquitoes now in retreat, the next invaders were the wasps, who had established several flourishing communities in the walls of the house and the pool. All day long they buzzed back and forth between their nests and the rich floral feeding grounds in the gardens. For a while, we just let them at it. They were a bit noisy, but we seemed to be able to coexist, and anyway, we were already fighting insect battles on several other fronts. Gradually, however, the numbers kept on increasing, until eventually we just couldn't go near the pool or sit on the terrace during the day.

The situation reached crisis point one Sunday afternoon when we were dining on the terrace with some French neighbours and their children. During the starters the wasps were annoying, but by the main course they had become completely intolerable – landing on our forks, scrambling across our plates, dive-bombing our drinks and basically running amuck. In the end, we just had to pack up and move inside. A few days later, Astrid was stung on the foot while playing in the garden. That was the last straw. They had crossed a line, the first shots had been fired, and another insect war was declared.

At first I felt pretty confident of victory. We had already outfoxed the ants and the mosquitoes and now I had a cunning plan for the wasps – simple but brilliant, like all great plans: I would mix up some plaster and simply fill up the holes in the walls, imprisoning the wasps in their own nests. I started with the nest in the wall of the house, but the entrance to the nest was tucked in behind one of the rafters of the terrace roof, which was a good three metres off the ground, so getting at it with plaster was not easy, not helped by the fact that the wasps were also constantly buzzing in and out. The best solution I could come up with was to place small balls of plaster on the end of a long wooden handle, which I then smeared onto the wall from a distance. With this ingenious method I managed to block the entire hole, and I looked on in triumph as a few returning wasps hovered around in confusion before eventually flying away again. I went to bed that night feeling good, maybe even a little cocky – never a good place to be!

The next morning, as I swaggered onto the terrace to check my handiwork, I was blindsided by a defiant, pucker-faced wasp that encircled me several times at close range, before flying up to the nest and entering through a newly created entrance. I looked on in disbelief – the rascals had burrowed through the plaster and reopened the nest. And so it was back to the war office.

With the enjoyment of the summer now in danger of being spoiled by unruly insects, I decided it was time for chemical warfare. I had been reluctant to use an insecticide before, as I really wanted to keep the premises as chemical free as possible, but the wasps had now become a real danger to children and adults alike, including paying guests in the gîte, so something decisive had to be done. At the hardware store in Prayssac I bought a large aerosol can of insecticide, which emerged as a white foam, a bit like shaving cream. It could be released through a nozzle and had a range of three to four metres, which meant I could stand well back and direct it towards the entrance of the nest. That evening I dosed the nest, or rather the entrance, as I couldn't get near enough to direct it inside. I repeated this every day for a week but it didn't make a blind bit of difference. The wasps simply carried on, perhaps looking whiter and fluffier than usual, but in no way less annoying.

The only bright spot on the horizon was the arrival of the hornets, a known predator of the lowly wasp. At first, we welcomed these giants as liberators, and despite their enormity and fierce-looking appearance, we were happy to have them around. But this soon turned out to be a case of the cure being worse than the disease, as they had almost no impact on the wasps, and in fact the hornets themselves soon became twice as big a problem as the wasps. They had an insatiable appetite for fruit, which probably explained their lack of interest in the wasps, and they completely ravaged the fruit trees, starting with the pears. The speed at which they could denude the trees was quite alarming, so much so that it spurred me into action on harvesting the fruit before it was all gone. Late one Saturday evening I set off for the orchard with an old wooden stepladder and a plastic bag, determined to salvage at least one good bag of fruit. I didn't have a lot of time as Tanya and I were going out that evening, and Anne was due to arrive any minute to mind the children.

I positioned the stepladder to give access to the higher branches where the biggest and ripest fruit could be found. Because it was so late, I was expecting that the hornets would have already called it a day, but as I climbed up nearer the top of the ladder the unmistakeable buzzing of well-juiced hornets got louder and louder. It was unnerving, like the sound of fighter planes, but I decided to press on cautiously. By the time I reached the second last rung there was some nice fruit within reach, so I started to fill the bag. I got around nine or ten pears and was reaching for another big one when, out of nowhere, a massive and viscous-looking hornet came straight at me. I ducked to the left, just barely avoiding a head-on collision, but, as I did, I lost balance and I felt the ladder moving off to the right, as I moved to the left. It felt like everything was happening in slow motion. I was falling, but I still had time to look towards the window, where I saw Tanya and Anne looking out at me. Still clinging on to the bag of pears, I tried to make it look like I was casually jumping down from the tree, but it didn't really work out, not helped by the fact that I landed on my side rather than my feet. Fortunately, I wasn't badly hurt – just some bruising, mostly to my ego.

I pulled myself up off the ground, picked up the few pears that had fallen out of the bag and shuffled off in the direction of the house. I entered the living room, expecting to be greeted with howls of laughter and abuse, but it turned out that neither of them had seen a thing. I knew Tanya's eyesight was not particularly good, and it turned out that Anne's wasn't so hot either. Just as well that I wasn't seriously hurt, or I might have been lying there for a while.

In the end, both the hornets and the wasps prevailed, despite our best efforts, as did the horseflies and the dreaded aouta bug (or harvest bug), an insect we had never heard of before we moved to France; if we had, we might have thought twice about it. A characteristic of this silent and almost invisible attacker is that it likes to play dirty, showing a particular preference for the genital areas. It is said that it is normally only found in long grass but, trust me, it is also to be found in short grass and even in places where there is no grass at all. The most annoying thing about being bitten by the aouta bug is that the itching can go on for a week or more before it finally starts to subside. It was a nuisance, but something we just had to put up with. There was no known repellent, and no treatment that we were aware of, so bar scorching the entire property, which did cross my mind once or twice, there was very little we could do.

Wallowing in defeat, and nursing bites from several different kinds of insects, we learned a valuable lesson during this first summer at Laborie: essentially, you just have to learn to live with nature, insects included. For some, such as the mosquitoes, you can take steps to control them, but in general you have to find a way to coexist. The wasps and hornets can pose a danger, especially to children, and sometimes have to be removed from areas close to the house, but it is possible to live with them, as long as you take certain precautions. The aouta bug is an even greater menace but again, appropriate clothing and regular hot showers can help to limit the damage. Over time, we learned to adjust and this really was the secret to survival in our new environment.

## 12

## *Tensions Rising*

Since we arrived in France, whenever possible I tried to start the day with an early morning walk. This has always been my favourite time of day, and it's especially nice in the country-side, and most especially in springtime. There is a quietness and stillness that you don't find at other times of the day, and it's the perfect time to gather your thoughts. There are also fewer insects around, which is an added bonus.

On the day Dave the builder was due to start the reno-vations, I confined myself to a short lap of the fields, as I wanted to be back at the house when he arrived. As it turned out, he didn't arrive until around 10.30 a.m., but given the problems we had already had with builders I was just happy that he arrived at all.

The first few days went okay, despite the late starts – it was usually 10 a.m. or later when he arrived, which was a bit annoying, and he never stayed past 4.30 p.m., even when he arrived late. But at least while he was on-site and work-ing things seemed to progress well, for a while at least. On the Monday morning of Dave's second week on the job, he arrived even later than usual, just after 11 a.m. I was in the kitchen when he came in and in a typical case of 'attack being the best form of defence', he complained about having to wait for the bathroom furniture, which, according to him, we were supposed to buy. I pointed out to Dave that the bathroom furniture had been included in his quote as something he would provide. He eventually conceded this, but then went on to argue that it would be better if we bought it, as we knew better what we liked, and he would allow us €100 off the quote, which is what he said he had estimated the cost at.

I had tried to like Dave. I really had. We didn't have too many friends in the area and we also needed a builder whom we could trust and rely on, especially as there was also going to be lots of other work to do. Unfortunately, my desire for good relations didn't seem to be reciprocated.

'Dave, €100 won't even buy us a toilet. Do you really expect that we can buy all the bathroom furniture for that?'

'Well, I was basing this on the cheaper options.' This was despite the fact that he previously told me he would 'never go for the cheapest options in bathroom furniture.' 'You can get a toilet for €20–30, a shower for about €50 and a hand-basin for another €20–30.'

'Maybe, if we were furnishing a doll's house Dave, but you know right well there's nothing, at least of any half-decent quality, at that price.'

The more the discussion went on, the more annoyed I felt. Finally, I had enough. I asked him for a revised quote, leaving out the materials, and I went back to work in my office. A few minutes later, Dave jumped into his van and raced down the avenue, spewing clouds of dust and dirt in his path. He told Tanya before he left that he would bring the quote the following day.

It was clear that things were now going south with Dave, and I anticipated further problems in the days ahead. It was frustrating, and at the end of the day I found myself, once again, looking in the mirror and not seeing a man who was living the dream. Instead, I saw a man who was ageing rapidly and sporting the grey hairs and crow's feet to prove it.

The next day we heard nothing from Dave, which I wasn't too surprised about, but I was concerned now that we might not hear from him again.

I wish I could tell you that just at this point, when everything was starting to look hopeless again, a saviour in the form of an expert, time-conscious and not overly expensive builder appeared on the horizon but, alas, this was not the case. What did appear on the horizon was a battered and rusting 1980s Toyota Corolla, with an equally battered looking occupant, Pierre, the tiler our English neighbour had recommended.

His entrance was announced by the loud humming of an exhaustless engine, an explosion of dust and the nauseating smell of engine fumes – it sounded and smelled more like someone trying to land a helicopter than park a car. A few minutes later, from somewhere in the middle of all this chaos, Pierre emerged, with a cigarette hanging from his mouth and a dirty grin on his face. Not quite the embodiment of the hero figure, Pierre was a small, skinny-looking chain-smoker, with a big mop of grey hair and a slightly bent posture.

As we exchanged greetings, I examined him closely, trying desperately to identify some features that might identify him as an able tiler, but I was at a loss. We walked on towards the house and, to my surprise, he went right through to the kitchen with the cigarette still in his mouth. Tanya was tidying up after breakfast and was shocked when she turned around to see him filling the room with smoke.

'*Bonjour Madame!*'

'*Bonjour Monsieur*, nice to meet you, but would you mind not smoking? We have young children and we don't like smoking in the house', Tanya explained in her politest French.

He didn't seem too impressed, but turned and flicked the cigarette back out through the front door. Unfortunately, however, as the smell of cigarette smoke subsided, certain other odours were unmasked. I could see Tanya's nose twisting and turning in discomfort, so I ushered Pierre back out of the kitchen and off in the direction of where the work had to be done.

He walked with a slight limp and, as we discussed the work, he also complained of having back problems and said he wouldn't be able to lift anything heavy. I was still hoping to be able to tick off at least one of the criteria that might qualify him for the job, but what I had seen and heard was not exactly filling me with confidence – a limping, chain-smoking featherweight with back problems, no qualifications and the general look of someone with an adversity to work. It didn't look good, but we had no alternative at this point, and he had been recommended – surely that had to count for something?

The big surprise, however, came a few days later, when I got his quote. Despite all his obvious handicaps, he still quoted more than double the amount of the fit-looking pro-fessional tiler we had earlier seen. Pierre, it seemed, was part of an opportunistic wing of the local building fraternity who took the view that expats had more money than sense. In fact, many of the quotes we received for building work during our first year in France were double and sometimes treble the normal rates (confirmed by our French neighbours and local trade associations). To satisfy myself that I wasn't being unfair in my assessment, I phoned an architect I knew in Cahors and asked him what the going rate for tiling was. He checked with the *chambres de metiers*, a kind of trade asso-ciation for the building professions, and confirmed a figure that was very close to what the professional tiler had quoted, which was less than half of what Pierre was looking for.

I phoned Pierre and told him what I had learned and that I wasn't happy with his price. He couldn't fathom the fact that I had gone behind his back to check prices like that, suggest-ing that he was in some way dishonest or underhanded, and he insisted that the information I received was all a load of bull anyway. What would those people know? This was just some body set up to regulate the industry and to stamp out malpractice – what business did they have talking to someone who suspected they were in danger of being overcharged? When he eventually realised that this line of argument was going nowhere, he attempted to justify his price on the basis of his crippling personal expenses – was I not aware that he had just built his own house and that he had to pay money to his ex-wife every month? At the end of this fairly bizarre justification, during which he must have realised how fool-ish he sounded, he suddenly agreed to halve his price.

With the professional tiler having already ruled himself out due to his busy schedule, it felt like we had little choice but to go with Pierre. He started the following Monday and basically it was trouble from the word go. He smoked all day long in the house, despite the fact that we asked him several times not to; he complained constantly about the weight of the tiles; he looked for money almost every day; and then, about halfway through the job, he arrived one morning and told me that he wanted an extra €3,000, on top of what he had quoted, or he would leave immediately. We already had enough of Pierre at this point, so in one way his ultimatum was music to our ears. Regardless, I didn't like being held to ransom like this, and an extra €3,000 was completely out of the question, so I told him it was a ludicrous demand and that if he wasn't prepared to stick to the original price then he was welcome to leave.

This wasn't the answer he had anticipated and it sparked off an unholy row. He yelled at me, complaining that the work was too difficult, that I shouldn't have asked him to do it in his condition, that his doctor had said he shouldn't be lifting anything heavy, that it was all my fault, and so on and so forth. When he finally paused for breath, I pointed out that if he wasn't supposed to be lifting then he shouldn't have taken the job in the first place, and I enquired as to why he was looking for more money to continue a job that he wasn't fit for. But the more I argued with him the more irate he got. He even threatened to call the tax authorities in Cahors 'to tell them what was going on'. He said he knew someone 'senior' in the tax office and would tell them what I was up to, employing people who were not registered. This made me laugh, as he was the only one on site who was not registered, and it was he himself who had insisted on being paid cash. But somehow, he also held me responsible for this, and for just about everything else that was wrong in his life. Having listened for as long as I could stand it, I finally asked him to leave, which he eventually did, but even as he left he still persisted with his hollow threats.

And so another day ended on a sour note. This really wasn't how we had envisaged our new life in France, and even though many of the expats I spoke to in the area had similar experiences with builders and tradespeople, nobody ever seemed to talk about it until it was too late. Maybe they were too embarrassed to admit they had problems, or maybe they were afraid of the possible repercussions of bad-mouthing local tradespeople. I'm not sure, but one thing I did learn from this experience was to beware of the recommendation.

## The Horse Fair

In May, Tanya's parents were coming to visit for the first time. The morning of their arrival, we set off early to pick them up at Toulouse airport. The kids were very excited about 'Mam' and 'Papy' coming to stay, so, against our better judgement, we kept them home from school and crèche that day to come with us.

The flight didn't arrive until early afternoon, but we had decided to make the most of the trip to Toulouse by taking in a quick visit to Ikea to pick up some last things we needed for the gîte. We got there just after 10.30 a.m. It was still relatively quiet, which was just as well as it meant there were less people around to witness the mayhem that was about to ensue. As soon as we got inside the front door, the children's eyes opened wide with excitement as they looked on in amazement at what must have seemed like a giant indoor adventure park. We moved briskly through the first five or six areas, mainly to avoid breakages, until we reached the café. The plan was to bribe them into cooperation with fruit juice and chocolate brownies. This seemed to work well, for about twenty seconds or so, until they started chasing each other around the café and Astrid careered into an elderly man who was carrying a tray of hot teas and coffees. The poor man swayed to the left, then to the right, and finally stabilised again with only a minor spillage. As he composed himself and wiped the coffee stain on his trousers, the perpetrator stood looking at him expectantly, patiently awaiting her absolution, which, unfortunately for her, never came. The French have a great ability to hold firm in situations like this.

We pressed on and somehow we managed to get what we wanted, and more – much more – but we were completely stressed out. Our last stop was the Ikea restaurant, where we were hoping for some decompression before going on to meet Tanya's parents but, once again, drama was hot on our heels. This time, the terrible two decided to play house underneath the table, which was fine for a while, until Ned tried to get out in a hurray and turned the table on its head, sending food flying in all directions. Seeing the look of horror on our faces, he attempted to defuse the situation by reassuring us that it was alright, that he and Astrid were just having 'a crazy day'. In truth, we were all having a crazy day, and it became even crazier when I suggested the need for stricter parenting, which Tanya immediately interpreted as an attack on her parenting skills. This wasn't what I meant, nor was it the time or place for such a discussion, which I realised as soon as I had said it. Inevitably, this led to an exchange of words and things were said that shouldn't have been said, and all the pent-up stress of the move suddenly came to the fore. We had reached a low point, possibly our lowest since our arrival in France. When the talking stopped, I looked at Tanya across the table and she looked spent. Her face was pale and thin, her hair was flat, and she just looked tired and unhappy. I'm sure I looked the same, and probably worse, as I certainly felt jaded, but seeing her like this made me feel annoyed and determined to do something about it.

We were supposed to be living the dream, making a better life for ourselves and our children, and here we were at each other's throats and feeling miserable. In a way, this moment had to happen. We had an expectation of our new life in France but the reality was very different, and somehow we needed to purge ourselves of the feelings of disappointment that were building up before we could move on. As we sat there, contemplating the situation, it started to dawn on me that we were probably trying too hard. We had become almost desperate to make our dream a reality and it was destroying us. We needed to step back and appreciate and enjoy what we had achieved and accept that not everything was going to be perfect, and that not everything had to happen straight away.

We made up, packed up and headed for the checkout, where we were duly told that we would have to drive to the depot 2 kilometres down the road to pick up the larger items. When we got to the depot, the larger items arrived, looking even larger than we had imagined. I asked an anxious-looking man at the information desk about the possibility of having the stuff delivered. He disappeared into a small office behind the desk and returned a few minutes later with his arms outstretched and a downturned mouth. I felt a cold chill running down my back.

'I'm sorry mister, but you're out of luck.'

With our first guests in the gîte due to arrive the following week, and all the furniture still to be assembled, we had no option but to try to fit everything in the car, which was already full. After much pushing and shoving and pressing and squeezing, somehow we managed to get everything in.

It was uncomfortable and dangerous, but we had no time to dwell on it: we were already late for Tanya's parents.

When we arrived at the airport, I offered to stay in the car with the children. I really didn't want to have to look Tanya's parents in the eyes and tell them they would have to sit on top of an *Ektorp* bed frame for the entire journey back to the house. Tanya went to fetch them in the arrivals hall and when they got back I could see the look of horror on her mother's face. She immediately insisted on getting a taxi. It would have cost around €200 but it probably would have been the sensible thing to do. Tanya was having none of it, however – we came to pick them up and pick them up we would. We started to unload and reload even tighter than before. An hour later, there were only two items left to go in – a small rucksack and my father-in-law's right leg, which was sticking out of the front passenger door. There were already four bags on the floor in front of him and two suitcases on his lap, so there was nowhere he could put his right leg. Fortunately, even at 74, he was still a very fit man, so he didn't seem to mind when I forced his leg in and jammed it against the inside of the door. I then drove on with the remaining small bag on my lap. It was insane really, but we laughed about it on the way home and when we finally reached the house we burst out of the car from all sides.

The next morning we woke with aches and pains but everyone was still in good spirits. Ned was thrilled to have his grandparents around and delighted in telling them, at least every half-hour, of his plans to get four animals: a boy deer, a pony, a bunny rabbit and a horsey, and the more he told everyone about this plan the more he worked himself into a state of high excitement. Astrid was equally excited and had even gone in search of her granny, and her granny's make-up bag, at first light – around 6 a.m.

It was now 12 May and the weather was still very unsettled. There had been a few nice days at the end of April but in general it was wet and the temperatures were well below average for the time of year. Undeterred, we decided to stick to a plan we had made the evening before to go to the horse fair at Cazals, a small village about 12 kilometres away. We were even toying with the notion of perhaps buying a pony, one of Ned's four must-have animals. We arrived in Cazals around 10 a.m. and the village was already choc-a-bloc with cars. The fair was taking place in some fields just outside the village and we managed to get a parking space not far from the entrance. I hadn't expected much and, for the most part, I wasn't disappointed. It was the usual mix of stalls selling everything from chainsaws and lawnmowers to candyfloss and sausage rolls. In fact, there was hardly a horse in sight. At least, not until we got to the back field, where there was a small gathering of horses and ponies and people who actually wanted to come to a horse fair, rather than a hardware fair.

I liked this part. It felt a bit like stepping back in time, as we left behind the cars, vans, tractors, 4x4s and hardware stalls for a small gathering of people and horses. When we arrived into this timeless space, a stout, heavily moustached man in a blue and red suit ambled through the crowd with a loudspeaker, announcing the imminent arrival of 'Laurent le Magnifique' in the parade ring. We didn't take much notice of this at first – we were too busy trying to organise pony rides for the kids – but then I got a glimpse of Laurent, riding majestically through the crowd on a fabulous white horse, and my curiosity was aroused. With his dark gypsy good looks, his white flowing shirt and tight black leggings and leather boots, Laurent had the look of some kind of medieval horseman, and he turned heads as he made his way to the parade ring. Once inside, he didn't disappoint, giving a master class in exhibitionism: riding backwards, working his way underneath the horse as it galloped at speed around the ring, and running with the horse and jumping across it from one side to the other. For some of his feats he was joined by a pretty young girl, also dressed in a glamorous white outfit, and, near the end of the show, a young boy of about ten or eleven, who must have been his son, as he looked like a miniature of Laurent himself, entered the arena. You could see that the boy was overjoyed to be sharing the stage with his hero and he proved to already be a pretty accomplished horseman himself. There was something magical about the father and son routine which really touched me. I was in awe of the close bond that existed between them and I wondered if I would enjoy such a relationship with my own son as he got older. Would he look up to me in the same way, show me the same respect? I hoped he would, but I knew it was something I could not take for granted. I just hoped it came to me as easy as it seemed to come to Laurent.

For the grand finale, Laurent rode in a standing position, straddling two horses. It was showmanship at its very best – close up, in a small arena. When you can hear the heavy breathing of the horses, feel the ground shake as they gallop past, and witness the concentration beneath the relaxed, smiling exterior of the performer, and the slight imperfections of the performance, there is something infinitely more real, more powerful and almost spiritual about the experience. It stayed with me for a long time afterwards.

After Laurent left the arena I looked at the others and they were all equally entranced. They knew they had witnessed something special, something you don't see every day. In a world obsessed with mass media and celebrity, it is hard to find this kind of experience any more. There seems to be the big stage or no stage and we are the poorer for it. We didn't buy a pony that day but I think we all enjoyed this small, rural horse fair much more than we had expected. It was a welcome smooth patch on what was still a very bumpy road to the dream life.

## A Custodian of Nature

On 17 May we dropped Tanya's parents back to the airport and, as we exited the car park to make our way home, the weather suddenly turned for the better again. By the time we arrived home, the temperature had climbed by almost 10 degrees. It looked like summer had finally arrived.

That evening I took one of my by now all too infrequent walks around the property. It was really beautiful, with nature at its very best. The warm, moist air felt good on my skin and the vivid green of the fields and woods, speckled with the reds, blues and violets of wild flowers, was a feast for the eyes. Underfoot, a network of animal tracks criss-crossed the entire property, providing ready-made walking routes, and here and there the evidence of a foraging wild boar or a resting deer could be seen from the disturbed earth or flattened grass. I felt honoured to be the owner of such a beautiful piece of land, although, strangely, I didn't really feel like the owner. Certainly the plants and animals didn't know we were the owners. For them, it was just their habitat, their home, and they had as much a claim to it as we did, if not more.

During this first summer we regularly spotted deer grazing in the fields, usually near dusk, but occasionally they could also be seen closer to the house, especially early in the morning. Once or twice we even found a brave young fawn nibbling on the lettuce plants in the garden, but we didn't begrudge him this little treat. There was plenty of lettuce to go around and Bambi, as we christened him, never seemed to overdo it, always leaving enough behind for the rest of us.

The wild boar were more difficult to spot and only seemed to come out in the dead of night. However, I did manage to get a few glimpses. One evening while out running on one of the old forest tracks that criss-cross the commune, I stumbled across an enormous beast just as I rounded a bend. Both of us stopped in our tracks and the big, tusk-bearing boar just stood looking at me. He was much taller than I would have expected, and a lot leaner, nothing like a domestic pig. I stood and watched, and he did the same. He didn't seem to be afraid of me, which unnerved me a little. He held my gaze for what seemed like an eternity, but it was probably no more than ten or twenty seconds. He then continued on his way, unrushed and seemingly unfazed by the whole experience.

My most memorable encounter, however, came in the early autumn, which is the rutting or mating season for deer. Every evening for about a week we had been hearing the sounds of stags bellowing in the hills and woods nearby. One evening the sounds seemed to be much closer than before, so I decided to go and investigate. I walked through a small wood at the back of the house, down a narrow lane and into an open field that was bordered by a larger wood at the far side. Once I was in the field I could hear the deep grunting sound coming from higher up in the woods. It sounded quite close and seemed to be getting closer all the time, so I decided to wait by the edge of the field.

As I stood, motionless, I could hear the bellowing getting louder and louder, and the heavy thudding of hooves getting closer and closer. Moments later, I heard the sound of branches breaking and it suddenly dawned on me that there was a very large animal heading in my direction. At this stage, I have to admit, I contemplated turning and running, but it seemed like too good an opportunity to miss so I swallowed hard and stood firm. The bellowing was now ending in a loud roar, and then suddenly an enormous stag burst through the thick scrub at the edge of the wood and walked out into the field. He must have been only about 20 metres from where I was standing. He was enormous, as big as a medium-sized horse, with immense antlers. It was definitely the biggest and most impressive animal I had ever seen in the wild. At first he looked agitated but he seemed to calm somewhat once he got out into the field. He surveyed his surroundings and I could see that he spotted me but, similar to my experience with the wild boar, he didn't seem particularly bothered by my presence. A few seconds later, he turned and disappeared back into the cover of the trees. The experience left me feeling quite humbled but also very privileged. I had no idea before this that such large animals were living in our woods. I hurried back to the house to tell Tanya and the kids, feeling a bit like David Attenborough, desperate to recount the story of my wild adventure.

The wild adventurer feeling didn't last long, however, as later that evening, still on a high from my deer-stalking expedition, I had a second encounter with a wild creature, this time with less impressive results. Tanya had just gone upstairs with the children and I was sitting alone in the living room when I heard some kind of grating noise. At first I thought it was a problem with the television, but when I turned down the volume I realised that the loud scratching sound was actually coming from the fireplace. I couldn't see what it was, as the previous owners had blocked off the front of the fireplace with a sheet of polystyrene in order to stop the draught, so I decided to make some noise myself, hoping I would scare away whatever it was. I coughed, stamped on the floor, shouted and made loud whishing sounds. There was silence for a few moments, until the grating started again, even louder this time. It seemed to be trying to scratch its way through the polystyrene and into the room, which really freaked me out altogether, despite my recent wilderness experience. I raced out of the room only to bump into my adoring wife, who had earlier been in awe of my stag stalking.

'There's something in the fireplace', I gasped, trying my best to appear calm and collected. 'I don't know what it is but it's big and it's trying to get out.'

Tanya came to the door of the living room and on hearing the noise ran back into the kitchen.

'Let's bring in Nipper', I suggested.

'No, we can't do that, it might attack him.'

'No, no, I'm sure it will be afraid of him, probably the smell of a cat will be enough to scare it.'

Tanya eventually consented to putting Nipper in the firing line, rather than her husband, so I gathered him up and slipped him through the living room door. He raised his nose to sniff whatever scent was in the air and then hurled himself back against the door. Tanya opened the door and he charged past us, back into the safety of the kitchen, the hair standing on his back.

'Oh poor Nipper, he looks terrified.' Tanya was now looking at me, indicating that it was my turn, but I didn't feel I was ready for this kind of challenge so we decided to call Lars. When he arrived, Lars pretended to hold back his laughter, as if he was trying not to make me feel like an idiot, but doing it at the same time.

'Where is this giant beast?', he yelled in his loud, theatrical voice.

Tanya showed him into the living room, while I pretended to be busy with something more important in the kitchen.

'Stand back, it could be a vile dragon', he boomed, as he marched towards the fireplace. He hesitated for a moment, looked around, and then picked up the poker. He stood with the poker raised above his head and then quickly ripped away the polystyrene board.

'Agggh …', he roared, as he plunged the poker aggressively into the fireplace. 'Got ya, got ya!', he shouted at the top of his voice, before thrusting the poker into the fireplace again, even harder this time.

He straightened his body again and, letting the poker fall by his side, he waved Tanya back in. 'It's okay now, you can come and have a look. This monster won't be bothering you again.'

'What was it? Are you sure it's dead?', said Tanya, as she inched forward.

Lars said nothing. Tanya crept towards him and held onto his arm as she peered into the fireplace.

'Aggh, it's still alive', he cried, jumping backwards and raising the poker again.

Tanya ran from the room, screeching at the top of her voice, as Lars burst into hysterical laughter.

'Just kidding! Don't worry. It's just a little beetle', he teased.

We both went back into the living room to have a look, relieved and slightly mortified.

'Don't worry guys. I know the noise of the scratching against the polystyrene can be really exaggerated. In fact the same thing happened to Mrs Sumner a couple of years ago.'

It really cheered me up to know that I was just as brave as a 75-year-old woman. However, there was hope for me yet – my aspiration of being the Irish Ray Mears might have taken a bit of a hit, but I was only down, not out. At least not until a few weeks later, when I really did deal myself a killer blow.

It was late in the evening and Tanya and I were watching television when we heard a noise on the terrace. I went to investigate, walking cautiously into the kitchen. The light was off, so I decided to take a look out through the window, but I couldn't see a thing. It was one of those pitch-black nights that you sometimes get in the countryside, where you literally cannot see two feet in front of you. I continued slowly into the hall, stopping to listen at the front door. I could hear the sound of something, or someone, moving around on the terrace. Then I got a whiff of something. It smelt like cigarette smoke. My heart was pounding in my chest at this stage. I slipped back into the living room and informed Tanya, in a low voice, that I thought there was someone outside.

'I can hear someone moving around and there's a smell of cigarette smoke.'

Tanya followed me back into the hall and sure enough, she heard and smelt the same thing.

'What are we going to do?', she asked expectantly, looking terrified.

I didn't really have an answer. Well, I did, but I just couldn't bring myself to say it, and, as it turned out, I didn't have to, Tanya did it for me.

'We have to call Lars!'

It was the last thing I wanted to do, but it was still better than being ransacked by a bunch of villains. Within a couple of minutes, Lars was at the front door, alone. There wasn't a sign of anybody or anything on the terrace, not even a humble beetle. We looked around the front of the house with torches, Lars leading the way of course, but there was no sign of man or beast.

'It must have been a dog. The big dog from the house down the road has been around our place at night; it was probably him', Lars suggested, trying once again to reassure us that he didn't think we were completely mad.

'But what about the cigarette smoke?', enquired Tanya, still not fully convinced.

'Not sure about that', said Lars. 'I haven't seen him smoking, but who knows. No, but seriously', he continued, 'sometimes the smoke from the wood here smells a bit like cigarette smoke, and when the wind is blowing in a certain direction, the smoke from your chimney is blown towards the front of the house.'

It sounded like a reasonable explanation, and one that allowed us to keep some sense of self-respect. The following night the 'villains' were back on the terrace, but they didn't smoke this time, and when I shone the torch through the window I discovered that the 'villains' were in fact a big brown dog, just as Lars had suggested.

Of course, the sound of a big dog rummaging around on the terrace was only a small part of the orchestra of sound that kicked off outside the house every night. There was all kinds of whooping and barking, and occasionally some pretty ferocious screeching. Clearly we weren't alone in our battle for survival.

# 13

# The Summer of Discontent

By the beginning of June, the weather had improved and was more in line with what we had expected, but it was only after a couple of weeks of this warm, sunny weather that we really began to appreciate how different the climate was to what we had known in Ireland or Belgium. In this part of Europe, in the summertime at least, it's normal for the sun to shine. Three consecutive days of sunshine don't spark off mass hysteria and wild speculation of heat waves or 'the hottest summer in decades'. Nor does it lead to frantic attempts to transform your skin colour from milky white to scarlet red in the course of an afternoon. Instead, there is a kind of relaxed assuredness that most days will be nice, so there's no need to panic or rush out and burn yourself into a cinder on day one.

But it's not just the fact that the sun shines more often, it also shines much more brightly. Countless writers and artists have commented on the brilliance of the light in this part of France but it's only when you experience it that you really understand what they mean. When the sun is out, even in winter time, every minute detail becomes visible, with a sharpness and clarity that I have never seen anywhere else.

Of course, there was always a danger, especially for us wind- and rainswept Irish, that as soon as the sun came out we would down tools and imagine that we were on holidays, so we needed the odd reminder that this was normal and that life had to go on; and unfortunately, there was no shortage of such reminders.

Jacques the farmer was one pretty constant reminder that we weren't on holidays, and at the beginning of June he struck again, when we found his cows trampling around our garden. I wasn't really that surprised, as he had been keeping them in a field that bordered the end of our garden and I had noticed a few days earlier that the grass had been eaten right down to the roots. In contrast, on our side of the fence there was a lush green meadow that must have looked like a royal banquet to the poor cows, so it was only to be expected that sooner or later they would step over the low-hanging fence, which wasn't even electrified, and into the banqueting hall.

When they did, they got so giddy with excitement that all they could do was run and jump and stamp and excrete all over their lovely feast. They then decided to march on the swimming pool, where their boisterous shenanigans continued. At one stage it looked like they might even knock each other into the pool. Fortunately, their noisy behaviour caught our attention just in time and Tanya and I set out with two sticks to herd them back to the desert from whence they came.

However, as soon as they realised what was going on they made a dart for the gate and the road beyond. By the time I reached the gate they were already 50 metres down the road and heading for the main district road, which was another 150 metres away. The district road could be quite busy at times so, despite my reservations about Jacques, in the interests of animal welfare I decided to alert him to what was going on. I jumped into the car and drove up to the village, where I found him standing on the terrace talking to his mother. When he heard the news he jumped into his car and sped off down the road without saying a word. His mother thanked me for letting them know. A short while later, I saw him driving the cows back up the road towards the village.

A few days after that they were back in the desert again, and a day or two later they were back in our garden. This time we were having lunch in the house and we weren't aware of what was going on until the people staying in the gîte brought it to our attention. Tony and Susan, a nice Australian couple, had been relaxing by the pool when they were suddenly surrounded by a herd of hungry cows. Susan, a glamorous-looking woman in her mid- to late fifties, managed to escape and ran up to the house to alert us to this terrifying situation. She looked petrified as she tried, between gasps, to describe how 'a bunch of great big cows' had attacked herself and Tony at the pool.

'Poor Tones is down there now, trying to fight them off', she explained.

Not wishing to see our first guests being eaten alive by vicious cows, I sprang from the chair and rushed to Tony's defence. From a distance, I could see him waving a chair above his head and yelling like a man who was fighting off a pack of wolves.

'It's okay Tony, they're not dangerous', I shouted. But Tony was 'in the zone' as they say, so it was difficult to get through to him. I ran across the garden, fearing that he might actually hit one of the cows with the chair, which would really stir things up with Jacques.

'It's okay Tony; we're going to get them out of there now.'

Tony put the chair down and suddenly gave the impression of being totally at ease with the situation. He even insisted on helping me move the cows towards the gate, although he did stand quite close to me, and jumped like a nervous kitten if the cows even looked sideways at him. This nervous twitching wasn't helpful, in fact, as it also made the cows uneasy, and after one particularly jerky reaction they scattered and ran in several different directions. Two of them went running down towards the woods at the bottom of the garden so I set out after them first, with Tony stuck to me like a conjoined twin.

On the way, we discovered a big hole in the ground at the end of the garden. In fact it was a miracle that one of us, or one of the cows, didn't fall into it, as it was completely screened with vegetation. It looked to be a good metre and half in diameter and even in the full light of day we had difficulty seeing the bottom. It could have been three or four metres deep. It wasn't a well, as there was no evidence it held water, and it was on the side of a slope. Rumour had it that this hole formed part of a tunnel that ran between two châteaux, one on a hill overlooking the village and another in a small hamlet to the south of the village. Apparently, our local village was on the front line during the Hundred Years War and the story goes that the tunnel facilitated secret communication between the two châteaux, which were in French control. Our house is located at the centre of a straight line between these two châteaux and, supposedly, there was also a prominent building on the site of our property at this time, so this theory didn't seem too far-fetched.

Whatever the truth of its origins, Tony was fascinated and intrigued, and it helped to take his mind off the cows, which had regrouped in a corner of the garden. While Tony took a closer look at the hole, I managed to get them back into the field and later that evening I informed Jacques and asked if he could ensure it didn't happen again, as it was upsetting our guests. To his credit, it didn't happen again, but it had not been a good start for our gîte business.

Fortunately, we were lucky with Tony and Susan, who were our first paying guests; they were good-humoured and incredibly tolerant, which were welcome, even necessary, characteristics, as just about everything seemed to go wrong during their stay. The problems started when they arrived the previous Sunday, a few hours earlier than we had expected. We probably should have told them that the gîte wasn't ready, but we were keen to make a good impression so we foolishly pretended that everything was fine. In reality, everything was far from fine. The pool was filthy, and naturally this was one of the first things they went to check out. Then Tony headed for the gîte and I could see Tanya's face tense up. I didn't really know what she was afraid of; I'm not sure she did either, but a few minutes later Tony reappeared holding a smelly bag of rubbish he had found under the sink, where he had also discovered evidence of recent mouse activity. To say there were red faces all round would be an understatement.

We tried to make excuses, blaming some friends who had stayed there for not putting out the rubbish, but it all sounded a bit hollow. Luckily, they didn't make a big fuss about it and we assured them it would be dealt with forthwith. An hour or so later I shuffled back from the pool, my entire body wet with sweat from frantic cleaning, only to find Susan in deep conversation with Tanya on the terrace. It looked like more trouble, so I tried my best to slip by without getting involved, but Tanya was wise to me.

'Eamon, Susan and Tony are having some problems with the washing machine and television, which don't seem to be working. Can you have a look?'

I must have looked like a man who had just been handed down a life sentence, as Susan immediately started to apologise for the trouble they were causing and insisting that it would be fine the next day. It was nice of her to say it, but deep down I knew that we really needed to get our act together – why should she be apologising? She was supposed to be enjoying her holidays. I assured her that it was no problem at all, despite my bedraggled appearance, and I accompanied her to the gîte straight away to see if I could sort out the problems. As I walked on ahead, trying my best to look purposeful, I was taking a mental note of the many things we needed to improve before our next guests arrived.

That night we had a lively discussion about the gîte, mutual responsibilities, what Tanya said, what I said, and so on. We were doing what many couples do when they are overworked, exhausted, stressed, in each other's company all day every day, and then something is cocked up – blaming each other.

The next morning, the atmosphere was pretty cool over breakfast. After cleaning the pool, I headed for my office to tackle some of the work that was now starting to mount up, but I had barely sat down at my desk when Tanya arrived in, asking if I knew anything about the cooker in the gîte – Susan had just been over again to say that they couldn't get it working. Around mid-morning, I took a break from my own work and I went down to the gîte to offer Susan and Tony the use of our barbeque and to apologise for all the problems but, true to form, they brushed it off as if it was nothing. Later than evening, while sitting down to have his aperitif, Lars, whom we had earlier consulted with on the cooker problems, had a brainwave. He suddenly remembered that the cooker in the gîte worked by convection, so we needed to use iron or magnetic pots and pans. Another crisis averted, and Lars was now well and truly on his way to sainthood.

## Bob the Builder

By mid-June we were basking in glorious summer sunshine, and *Bob the Builder* had just overtaken *Balamory* as Ned and Astrid's new favourite cartoon. It's quite possible that this sudden fascination with the construction industry was somehow influenced by the real-life building site drama that was being played out all around us on a daily basis, which would have made quite good cartoon material in its own right.

Having departed under a dark cloud a few weeks earlier, our own Dave the Builder had returned, this time with a team of handymen, who included his brother, James, a skinny young lad with an enormous mop of black hair, and his friend, Tommy, who looked and sounded a bit like Paul Gascoigne. The odd thing about this trio, however, as opposed to Bob the Builder's crew, was that none of them seemed to have the foggiest idea how to build anything. They knew how to talk the talk, especially Tommy, who seemed to have an opinion, and sometimes a fairly warped one, on just about everything – from how to make a good cup of tea to how to run your car on tractor diesel.

Their lack of progress wasn't helped by the fact that it was getting later and later when their battered blue van rolled into the yard every morning. They were also leaving early. On 23 June, they left immediately after lunch as they wanted to go home to watch England playing in the World Cup. Annoying as this was, we could probably have lived with it, at least that was until the end of the week, when Dave presented us with an invoice for five full days of work for all three of them. It was the same story the week after, which included one day that he supposedly spent in Montauban, picking up materials. This was a round trip of two hours, but Dave had the audacity to look for a full day's pay.

We muddled through these difficulties, but our relationship was on a downward spiral again and it got to the point where we just wanted him gone, as quickly as possible. Unfortunately, we didn't have any other options and, as we were already at the beginning of the tourist season and needed to get the B&B finished, we were stuck with him, but it was costing us dearly, both financially and psychologically. Because of all the time-wasting and short days, the bill was also starting to mount up, which on top of the many other unforeseen expenses was putting a strain on our finances.

## In the Eye of the Storm

On Friday 2 July, things finally came to a head. After another week of late starts, early finishes and lots of cock-ups in between, we had had enough. When Dave presented me

with the usual bill for five full days of work I shared with him
my record of the hours worked and offered to pay him for
four days. It was a confrontation that was long overdue and
I knew there was only one possible outcome, but we weren't
prepared to put up with any more of Dave's baloney, and I
told him so. He didn't like it but, strangely, he didn't seem
to have the words to explain why. Instead, he gathered up
his motley crew and stormed off in a huff. As I watched the
back of the van disappear down the lane I felt a great sense
of relief, followed moments later by an even greater feeling
of anxiety. We didn't have to put up with Dave any more, but
now we had a deserted building site on our hands, and there
was still a lot of work to be done. By the time I got back to the
house I was feeling alone and dejected. Tanya was sitting at
the kitchen table, holding her head in her hands. She looked
at me and we both forced a smile. We didn't have to say anything; we both knew the predicament we were in.

That night I lay awake, wondering what to do next. Every
day seemed to bring new problems and worries. It wasn't
meant to be like this. We were supposed to be enjoying an
easier and less stressful life, spending more 'quality' time
with our children, and having more time for hobbies and
the good things in life, but it wasn't working out like that. I
twisted and turned, trying to convince myself that everything
would be fine, but the little voice in my head kept telling me
otherwise. Eventually, probably exhausted from the endless
analysis, I must have momentarily nodded off to sleep, as I
was suddenly thrust back into a state of semi-consciousness
by what sounded like a bomb exploding about six inches
from my head. The whole room lit up, and a few seconds
later there was another terrifying explosion.

For a few seconds I lay there, half asleep and half awake,
trying to figure out what was going on. My sleepy, dreamy
half was telling me that World War Three had just begun,
while my conscious, wakeful half was telling me that I was just
dreaming. After another succession of deafening explosions I

was fully awake, and experiencing a storm the likes of which I had never experienced before. The thunder was almost deafening, and coming from directly overhead. A few times I was certain the lightning must have hit the roof. It was a surreal experience. With every loud clap my heart jumped. Each time I hoped it was the last, but it continued for at least an hour and the lightning was so intense that it seemed like we were continuously switching between night and day. Tanya, amazingly, slept through the whole thing, as did the kids. The capacity of all three of them to sleep really astounds me sometimes, and is so different to my own light sleep patterns.

As soon as the thunder and lightning stopped, the rain started. At first it sounded like heavy rain, but it continued to gather momentum and before long it was sounding more like a torrent, and certainly the heaviest I had ever heard. It was absolutely bucketing down. I lay in bed listening, and counting my blessings that I was somewhere warm and dry, when all of a sudden I heard the sound of water dripping. It was slow at first but then it got faster and faster, until it eventually became a constant dribble and then it just sounded like someone had turned on a tap.

I couldn't quite make out where it was coming from, but then Ned started to cry and when I got to his room I found him sitting under a waterfall. The water was pouring from the ceiling and the poor chap didn't know what was happening. We had to haul him out of his soaking bed and dry him down with towels. While Tanya was doing this, I went up to the room over Ned's, which was the highest room in the tower, to see if I could locate the source of the problem. From there, I could see the water pouring in from the ceiling above. I ran to check my office in the other tower (now cursing the fact that we had to have a house with two towers) and found the same thing. And if that wasn't bad enough, there was more water flowing in under the windows.

I grabbed some towels from the bathroom and threw them on the floor, before running back to Ned's room with a bucket and more towels. On the way, I took a detour to the kitchen to pick up a torch, as by now the electricity had gone. When I got back to Ned's room I was confronted with yet another worrying sight – several neat little piles of sawdust forming just beneath the stairs to the upper level. On closer examination I noticed that quite sizeable holes were being eaten into the stairs just above the piles of sawdust; then the penny dropped – termites!

I went to bed about an hour later, having gone beyond the point of exhaustion. The water was still pouring in, the storm was still in full tilt, and now we also had to come to terms with the prospect of having termites, those nasty creatures that I had heard could literally eat an entire house in a matter of days.

I woke the next morning around 6.30 a.m., still feeling stressed from the night before. We had a rented van that had to be dropped back to the Leclerc supermarket by 8.30 so, after breakfast, Ned and I set off for Cahors. Ned was thrilled; it was the first time he had ever travelled in a van, and his first time in the front seat of anything. I was just shattered, but still glad of the opportunity to get away from the house for a while. On the way, I turned on the radio to learn that in nearby Provence the storm had claimed the lives of twenty people, with another twelve seriously injured. This really put our problems in perspective – we were all alive and well, and Ned was beside me having the time of his life. It was a well-timed reminder of the need to focus on the positives and on the big picture, and to try to see beyond the litany of petty problems that were starting to get me down.

I used to consider myself a lucky person. Things always seemed to work out pretty okay for me but, for some reason, since we moved to France, trouble seemed to follow me around like a bad smell. In fact, I now woke in the morning expecting something to go wrong before the day was out. Maybe I was just becoming French, I thought, since, according to a very wise French neighbour, it's normal for the French to get up in the morning expecting trouble. They embark on the day having prepared themselves for at least three confrontations before nightfall. This, he explained, is why the French are so highly strung. They are basically ready to fly off the handle at a moment's notice. My goal in life had always been to avoid confrontation where possible; to get through the day without a run-in is my definition of a good day. But when you live among a population of 60 million people who are collectively looking for around 180 million confrontations every day, I guess the odds are stacked against having too many days like that.

So when we arrived at Leclerc, just before 8.30 a.m., it wasn't all that surprising that a bit of argy-bargy was on the cards. Having completed the paperwork at the van rental desk, we accompanied a thin, pale fifty-something-year-old French woman to the car park for the customary inspection. I'm always a bit nervous in these situations as you just never know what they might try to pin on you, but on this occasion I was at least reassured by the fact that we hadn't had an accident or caused any damage, so I wasn't expecting too many problems. Accompanying me, however, was a French woman who had at least three confrontations to fit in before the day was out, and it looked like she was planning on having it pretty much wrapped up by mid-morning.

We had barely started the inspection when she spotted a large indentation on the back of the van, in the top left-hand corner. It looked like somebody had beaten it in with a sledge hammer, or, em … maybe reversed into something.

'It wasn't me', I pleaded, protesting my innocence. But as far as she was concerned she had me by the short and curlies – it was an open and closed case. Pointing to the chart from the last inspection, she insisted that the dent wasn't there before I took the van.

'It's a mistake, we must have missed it', I argued.

'No, no and no', she snapped, waving her documents in my face.

The stand-off continued all the way through the inspection, and back at the rental desk I refused to sign a form admitting responsibility. Despite how it looked, I was convinced the van hadn't been damaged while we had it. She pushed the documents at me again, but I still wouldn't sign them. With neither side willing to cede defeat, she eventually withdrew the forms and snarled at me that her boss would take it up with me the following Monday. I left the place completely wound up, and I remained like that for most of the day. But of course it was all a storm in a teacup, as I never actually heard from her boss. In fact, I never heard from either of them again.

Having escaped the clutches of this disagreeable woman, Ned and I dutifully went about our other chores of the morning. Top of the list was some kind of termite treatment. I had done a quick Google search before we left that morning and found the address of a shop in Cahors that seemed to special-ise in termite problems. When we arrived at the shop, I was reassured by the sign over the shop window: '*Traitement anti-termites*'. Now, my French is not fantastic, but that seemed pretty clear to me; of course, in life, and especially in rural France, things are not always what they seem. A few minutes later we were standing face to face with the shop assistant, who looked me in the eye and told me that he didn't deal in anything to do with termites. I laughed and suggested that it was a strange choice of name for a shop that had nothing to do with termites, but he didn't seem to find it strange, or funny for that matter. He looked at Ned and shrugged his shoulders, as if to say is your dad always like this?

I wanted to question him further, but after the run-in I had already had with the woman in Leclerc, I didn't have the energy or the inclination, so we left without any further discussion. I still don't know what kind of a shop it was. All I could see on the shelves were bags of some kind of grain or sand or something. I have no idea really. Fortunately, on the way home I had a call from Lars, who had just been over to the house to check out the damage, and he had some good news on the termites. In fact, he didn't think there were any termites. His theory was that the damage was being caused by something called the Capricorn beetle. I had never heard of the Capricorn beetle before but he assured me that it was much more preferable to termites and easily treated with a product called Xylophene.

He had some further news on the flooding situation, which he thought was a freak incident due to the direction of the rain rather than a leak in the roof. Apparently, it had happened at least once before that he was aware of, when the rain came from the south and penetrated the small openings in the top of the towers, so he reckoned it was just the direction of the rain and nothing to worry about.

Two pieces of good news in the space of five minutes – it was almost too good to be true. When I got home, there had also been a call from Dave the builder to say that he would be back the following week to finish off the work, and he just wanted to be paid for four days for the previous week. It just kept getting better and better!

## 14

## *Half-Baked*

Towards the end of July, peace broke out, and we enjoyed a welcome but unusual period of calm. The weather was good, the building work was finished and the gîte was occupied; the only minor hiccup was the cooker breaking down, but this hardly registered as an inconvenience in comparison to the difficulties we had already overcome. The cooker was the last of the old appliances left behind by Mrs Sumner; the others had all given up the ghost shortly after we moved in. It had been easy enough, and not too costly, to replace the dishwasher, washing machine and fridge. Most of the big chains had good deals on these kinds of items. The cooker was a bit more complicated, however, partly because the range on offer seemed to be much more restricted, but also because Tanya wasn't looking for any old standard cooker – she had her mind set on a top-of-the-range model, which was understandable, as it would also be needed for the B&B.

It was possible to find such an item, but at a gargantuan price, and because it just wasn't in my genetic make-up to pay €5,000 for a cooker, a bargain was going to have to be found somewhere. But such bargains were thin on the ground and after a few days of searching, while living on raw food, we were almost ready to throw in the towel and go for a bog standard, run-of-the-mill cooker. It was at this point that Anne intervened, informing us of a factory shop in nearby Duravel that sold end-of-line or slightly damaged appliances at knock-down prices. It was music to our ears, and before you could say 'hot dinner' we were in the car and pelting along at a lively pace towards Duravel.

It was a small shop and the selection wasn't fantastic but that didn't matter too much, as by some stroke of luck it just happened to have the deluxe model that Tanya was looking for. It was a Smeg, which she assured me was a top brand that ticked all the boxes. More importantly for me, it ticked the affordability box, coming in at a very reasonable €650. Happy days! Recognising the bargain that was staring us in the face, I stuffed a bundle of Euro notes into the shop assistant's hand, insisting on how much we liked the cooker and how we would love to have it delivered later in the day. In fairness, he did do his best to make this possible, but in the end we had to settle for a next-day delivery. We weren't too upset about this – we got what we wanted and one more night of raw carrots and canned tuna was a small price to pay.

The next morning, the delivery van rolled into the yard around 10.00 a.m. and the two occupants – a large, portly man in his early fifties and a tall, thin lad of about sixteen – leaped out, looking lively and energetic. They had the whole thing unpacked, in the house and installed in about half an hour, at which point the older guy, now stripped down to his white string vest and sweating profusely, retired to the terrace for a cigarette. Meanwhile, his eager companion, known only as 'the apprentice', ran through the finer points of the operating manual with Tanya. Before wrapping up this little briefing, he emphasised one point in particular – she needed to turn on the grill to the maximum for about thirty minutes, with the oven door open, to allow the toxic coating to burn off.

Toxic coating? That sounded a bit worrying, but as it turned out, it was more than the toxic coating that was a problem.

The nice shiny plastic knobs, located just above the oven door, also got a serious roasting and ended up in a droopy, downward position. By the time we noticed it, the two men were well gone, but the older man dropped back later in the evening with a piece of gas tubing they had forgotten earlier, and when we showed him what had happened he looked perplexed. When we explained what his apprentice had advised, he went ballistic: cursing about how the young lad was good for nothing, and how he was going to call around to his house that very evening and 'burn his knob', to see how he would like that. I had the distinct impression 'the apprentice' had form, and it seemed like his mentor was running out of patience. When he finally calmed down a bit he apologised for all the inconvenience and promised he would be back the following day with a new cooker. The next morning, the two men arrived back with a new cooker and removed the faulty one. The apprentice was still in one piece, although he did seem to be walking with a funny gait – or maybe I was just imagining it.

## Friends or Customers?

The good weather continued right through to the end of July and, as if that wasn't good enough, we were back eating cooked food again. On top of that, we were looking forward to the arrival of some friends from Ireland. This was one of advantages of having tourist accommodation, that we could now have friends out to stay more often, but there was just one minor complication, and I'm sure everyone who goes into the B&B or self-catering business grapples with this issue, and it's something we laboured over long and hard, even before we moved to France: whether or not to charge friends.

With family there was never any question of charging, but the numbers were manageable and we could usually accommodate them in the main house, especially if it coincided with bookings. Friends were another story. Firstly, we were fortunate enough to have accumulated quite a few friends over the years, and if they all decided to visit, for free, we could have been the busiest and most insolvent tourist business in France. Secondly, we were actually relying on this network of friends to generate business, particularly in our first few years. In the end, for better or worse, we decided to go with the policy that family would be free and friends would pay but we would offer them a discount. We thought this was a good compromise.

The arrival of our friends from Ireland was going to be the first real test of this discount policy. They booked into the B&B for two weeks, and at the same time some friends of theirs, whom we didn't know, also booked into the gîte. Our friends, John and Deirdre, and their children, Alison (5) and Jack (2), arrived first. We hadn't seen them for almost two years so it was great to catch up. The other guests arrived the following day, and as the week progressed we were all getting along swimmingly.

I was working by day most of the time, which I felt uncomfortable about, but I had no choice. If I took holidays every time we had friends or family visiting I would never have gotten any work done.

But I was really enjoying my time away from the office and work, and, as the week wore on, and the more convivial things got, the more uncomfortable we felt about charging John and Deirdre. I had met John at university, so I had known him for almost twenty years and, as we rekindled our friendship, it just felt wrong. At the end of the first week, as Tanya and I lay awake in bed, mulling over how things were going, I told her how I felt. Luckily she felt the same way, so we revised our plans and decided not to charge anything. The next day, I told John. He seemed genuinely surprised and completely disagreed, insisting that they wanted to pay and that it was only fair. But I stuck to my guns and refused to even discuss it any further; we had made our minds up and that was it. Tanya and I felt more relaxed after that and during the second week it really was more like having friends to stay. The awkwardness we felt the week before was gone. Our policy hadn't really worked as expected. Really, there was no right or wrong approach; we were just going to have to take it on a case-by-case basis.

A few days after their departure I had a call from John, who was now back in Ireland. We chatted about the holidays, which we both agreed had been great fun and something we should do more often, and then he asked me if we had found the envelope.

'What envelope?', I enquired.

'You didn't find it then. Have a look under the sink in the bathroom', he said, insisting that they would never stay with friends for two weeks without contributing something. For them it was a holiday and they expected to pay. Sure enough, when I checked the bathroom the envelope was sitting snugly wedged under the sink. Inside was a bundle of €50 notes which amounted to the original amount we had quoted. I still felt a little uncomfortable taking money from friends, but it was true that we had spent quite a bit on breakfasts, lunches, dinners and alcoholic beverages over the two weeks, so maybe I was being overly sensitive.

§

On the last weekend of John and Deirdre's two-week stay we had some more friends and family arriving, as we had planned a small christening party for Astrid. On the Friday afternoon I went to pick up my parents at Toulouse airport, and later that evening Tanya's brother and his girlfriend also arrived, along with another friend, Jane, a Unitarian minister. Tanya's parents had already arrived a few days earlier. That night we all went for dinner at La Recreation, a very nice restaurant in the pretty village of Les Arques, about 10 kilometres away. It was great to see everyone and we probably celebrated a little more than we should have, especially as the main event was due to take place the following day.

I struggled to get out of bed the next morning but we had a christening party to organise and there was a lot to be done. When I got downstairs, Tanya was already busy in the kitchen, and her mother joined her there a short while later. Meanwhile, Jane had descended from her bedroom at the top of the tower and, not looking at all well, headed straight for the terrace to write her sermon. As well as all the Irish gang, we had also invited Anne and her husband, Dominique, Lars and Helena, and Emily, our estate agent. It was an outdoor affair, so just after midday we all gathered in the corner of the garden and Jane kicked off the ceremony.

Afterwards, we made our way back to the terrace for aperitifs. We had set up a long table on the terrace, big enough to accommodate our 27 guests. We kicked off with champagne, which Tanya's father poured liberally and frequently. I abstained, and set about preparing the starters, which was my main responsibility in terms of the catering. We kept it simple – wild Atlantic smoked salmon with bruschetta – but, even so, plating up for so many people was a bit of a panic. Then came the main course, the *pièce de résistance*: two experienced cooks, three days of preparation and a budget to match a king's ransom.

As we waited in eager anticipation, an air of uncertainty emanated from the kitchen, so I decided to go and investigate. I was barely inside the door when I was handed a tray and ordered to start loading up plates – the pressure was on. The centrepiece, chicken in white wine vinegar sauce, had just come out of the oven and the two cooks were in a state of high excitement, trying to get it onto the plates and served while it was still piping hot. They were going for perfection, and nothing less would do. With the guests served, I went back into the kitchen to serve myself, but then Emily came rushing in behind me, carrying her plate in her hand and looking slightly distressed. She gathered the two cooks in close, and I could hear her whisper:

'I don't mean to cause a big fuss but my chicken seems to be a little pink.'

Tanya looked at her in disbelief, and then they examined Emily's plate.

'Oh God, that's awful. Yes, I can see it's not properly cooked. Let's have a look here and see if we can find you another piece.'

But it was the same story – all the pieces were pink!

With visions in my head of ambulances and guests being rushed to hospital with food poisoning, I ran to the table and began whisking plates from under people's noses. Meanwhile, the two devastated cooks tried to hobble together a credible substitute, to at least ensure that people didn't go hungry and had something to soak up the large quantities of champagne and wine that had already been consumed. I think nobody went hungry, but it was probably too late for the soakage to have any effect, and, as the evening progressed, things got quite animated. At one stage I noticed one of the female guests holding hands with Tanya's dad while singing the praises of Viagra, the wonder drug.

By the following Monday, everyone had left except for my parents, who were staying on for another week. It was nice having a full house, but it was also nice to have some calm again. We also had more guests arriving to the gîte on the Wednesday evening, so the grass cutting, pool cleaning and other chores, which had been on hold for a few days, all had to be tackled as a matter of urgency.

## Purple Haze

The rest of the summer sped by at breakneck speed as we struggled to stay on top of all the different jobs that needed doing. The children were also on their school holidays and my consultancy work was much busier than I had expected, which was a blessing in one way, as we really needed the money, but a challenge also, as I had so many other things to do.

As the summer came to a close, we took stock of how things had gone. From a business perspective, it really couldn't have gone much better: the gîte had been booked right through from mid-June until mid-September, and there was a steady stream of guests to the B&B all summer, despite the fact that we only started advertising in April. We had also met some really interesting people and, maybe it was just beginner's luck, but we had no complaints and lots of compliments. When there were problems nobody really blinked an eye – they were always forgiving, and usually turned it into an opportunity to chat and find out a bit more about our move and our new life in France. It seemed that just about everyone who stayed with us was considering a similar move, some probably more seriously than others, so there was a real curiosity about our situation: why we had moved, why we had chosen the Lot, how it was working out financially, and so on. Most of our guests were professionals, looking for a few weeks of peace and quiet, away from the demands of their lives back home, and this was something we were able to offer them in spades.

The social interaction with the guests was an aspect we hadn't really considered beforehand, especially as we had planned to focus mainly on self-catering, so we didn't expect that much contact, but there was quite a bit and we were surprised at how much we enjoyed it. We felt fortunate to have guests who were genuinely nice people and on several occasions we even invited some of them to join us for a drink in the evening time. On the whole, we had a really nice mix of guests: some people preferred more time to themselves, while others appreciated a bit more attention, and we learned to gauge this as we went along. This was also fine for us, of course, as while we like to mingle with the guests, we also appreciated some time to ourselves.

As autumn approached, it was time to put the summer behind us and prepare for winter. We were warned by our neighbours that winter could be very cold and very quiet in this part of France but, like all such warnings, you have to experience it yourself to really appreciate what lies behind the words.

# 15

# Easy in Autumn

During the very easy transition from summer to autumn, we started to find a more pleasant rhythm. The gîte had become easier to manage, and because we were on the last bookings of the season there was less pressure to maintain every-thing in tip-top shape. My consultancy work was also a little quieter, which meant I was less stressed and better able to enjoy the work outdoors and the time I had with Tanya and the kids.

The children started back to school and crèche in September and they both seemed to be settling in well, which was a real relief. It had taken Ned a few months to adjust, mainly because of language problems. However, by the end of the school holidays he had made huge strides and was much more confident in speaking and interacting with the other children.

With the easier pace of life, we also started to find time for other activities, the kinds of things that had attracted us to rural France in the first place. One Sunday towards at the end of September, for instance, we went on one of the regular walks that the local festival committee (*comité des fêtes*) organised. The entire commune is criss-crossed with little country lanes and winding paths that meander through the forests and pastures, perfect walking routes. On this particular day, the guided walk took us on a circular route, leaving from the village, passing through two small hamlets and then back to the village again, where a beautiful picnic lunch awaited us. It was the first time we went along on one of these walks and we had some reservations, even though we loved walking and had regularly gone on walking and hiking trips before the children were born. Our main concern was communication. Not speaking French fluently can be a real handicap in situations like this, and we expected that most of the group would be local French people. For this reason, we feared a slight awkwardness and expected to find ourselves more on the periphery rather than mingling with the group, but we persisted anyway as we felt that it was important to make the effort. As it happened, there were some language difficulties, and even a few solitary moments, but it still turned out to be a quite enjoyable occasion, helped also by the glorious weather and the breath-taking views of the countryside.

This part of France clearly had a glorious past – the countryside is dotted with châteaux, manors and some very fine farmhouses – but it seems to have been asleep for the past hundred years or more. Nature has reclaimed much of the land, which was once used to grow vines or to graze animals, with the result that most of the area is now forested. This extensive oak forest looks like it has been there for an eternity, but every now and again a glimpse of the area's past emerges – a protruding stone structure, an abandoned stone hut or dilapidated wall, or some other hint of human activity, barely visible through the trees or the forest floor, but opening up a small window to the past.

Apart from the magnificent scenery and the glorious weather, the people we met on the walk were the real icing on the cake, and it was probably a turning point in terms of how we felt about the area generally. Before, and even after we moved to France, people would often warn us that the French are not keen on foreigners and prefer to keep to themselves. In general, this has not been our experience. It is true that many French people we have come across are a little more reserved than, say, Irish people, but once you do make their acquaintance they can be just as warm and friendly. Many of our French neighbours clearly enjoy the company of foreigners and, barring odd mutterings from one local individual, whom nobody really takes any notice of anyway, we have never experienced even a hint of any ill will. This is not to say that such feelings do not exist in France, but it is not something that we have experienced. So as we wandered through the countryside, we chatted with Jean and Christine, who lived in Normandy but had a second home just outside the village; Florence, a friendly and feisty septuagenarian, who took charge of the kids for part of the walk, enthusiastically teaching them about the wonders of nature; and Andrea and Simona, who were originally from Italy but had lived in the area for over forty years and were now the life blood of the village seniors' club. They even used the opportunity to invite us to take part in some of their activities, including chess, crochet, boules, gourmet tours and yoga. We also had the opportunity to rest our brains with some lighter English conversation with Jim and Lynn, two long-time residents of the area, and the only other native English speakers on the walk.

Through these exchanges we learned a lot about our new neighbours, and they about us. We didn't come away from it feeling like we had cracked it, but it did feel like we had moved a step closer to being accepted members of our little community. I was really glad we had made the effort and for the first time in my life I had the feeling we were starting a process – and I expected it would be a long one – of putting down roots. When we finally entered the village at the end of the walk, which lasted about two hours, several long tables were laid out with the finest of local charcuterie, cheeses, fruit, fresh bread, and sturdy jugs of red and white wine. Why can't life always be like that?

§

It was also during this autumnal period that we instigated Friday night film watching with Lars and Helena. They had previously suggested this as a good way of keeping in touch, especially during the 'cold and lonely' winter months. We didn't expect much in the way of coldness or loneliness but we were keen anyway on the idea of watching some good films, and Lars and Helena had a huge collection that they were more than happy to share with us. The plan was that they would come to our place, avoiding the need for a babysitter, we would eat something, taking turns to prepare it, and then we would sit down to watch a film. On the first night, however, we ate and talked non-stop for three hours, so we had to postpone the film until the following week. The next Friday night followed a similar pattern, as did the Friday night after that, and the one after that. In fact, to this day we still haven't watched a film together, and maybe we never will, at least not on 'film night'. Instead, Friday nights became more about good food and good conversation, with two people who by now had become good friends.

## The Ice Age

Throughout October and November the good weather con-
tinued, with temperatures consistently in the high 20s. By the end of November I was beginning to wonder if we were going to have any winter at all. Then suddenly, on 1 December, all that changed. Temperatures plummeted by 15 degrees overnight and we went from what felt like summer to the depths of winter in a matter of hours. This cold snap continued right through to the middle of December, by which time night

temperatures had fallen to minus 15 degrees Celsius, colder than we had ever experienced before, and the coldest it had been in the Lot for several decades.

To coincide with these record low temperatures, our central heating system decided to shut down, late one evening, when we had no chance of getting a repair man. After several calls and much pleading with the woman in the local heating shop, we managed to get a technician out the following morning. Shuffling ahead of him, looking a bit like the Michelin Man on account of the number of shirts, sweaters and coats I was wearing, I showed him to where the oil burner was in the basement. He tried a few switches but nothing happened. He then strolled over to the fuse box on the wall and flipped the trip switch, before returning to try it again. To my delight, and utter disgust, it started up. With my limited French I tried to persuade him that there must have been something else wrong, that I had already tried the trip switch, but he was having none of it. He brushed past me and went on his way.

An hour later it cut out again and, having made certain it wasn't the trip switch, I called the shop again. This time I was told that Julian, the technician, would call to us on his way home, at around 6 p.m. He arrived on time and I got the impression he didn't expect to be with us for too long. Two hours later he was still there, sitting on the cold concrete floor in front of the oil burner, scratching his head. He had tried just about everything but to no avail. He still couldn't pinpoint the problem. I got the impression he was on the verge of giving up, so I went upstairs and made some coffee, hoping that would keep him going for another while. It was around 11 p.m. when he eventually got the boiler going again, but it must have been some kind of make-shift solution, as the next morning it stopped again. And this is how it continued for the rest of the winter: it would run for a couple of hours and then cut out, so we kept having to switch it on, and every morning we got up to a freezing cold house.

§

We looked into several options for improving the heating situation in the house, including installing a stove, changing the boiler, insulating the attic and changing our draughty, single-glazed windows to proper double-glazed ones. We eventually proceeded with the attic insulation, but because of chimney complications the stove solution had to be postponed, and the price of a replacement boiler, especially one fuelled by some kind of renewable energy source, was just prohibitive.

The double-glazed windows were also very expensive, not helped by the fact that we had around twenty that needed replacing, so we decided to investigate a system for adding a second panel onto the existing single-glazed windows, called *survitrage*. We found a company that specialised in this in the phonebook so we gave them a call and we were told that a representative would be in our area the following week.

Mr Didier, the representative, was loud and he laughed a lot, even when there was nothing to laugh at. He was the stereotypical travelling salesperson. I had already met quite a few at this stage, and I have met many more since, and I'm convinced they must all go to the same school, as their methods are so similar. Basically, it's a war of attrition. From the firm handshake to the lecturing and the bullish eagerness to dominate the conversation, the whole purpose seems to be to wear you down to the point where you just can't resist any more. Most of them carry a folder full of technical and financial details about their product or service, every bit of which they have to explain in full. After an hour or so of this, you can actually start to feel slightly delirious. It's like death by a thousand boring facts.

But there was one fact that Mr Didier refused to divulge and that was the price. I had asked for this repeatedly during his presentation, hoping to save us all some time, but he completely ignored me every time, ploughing ahead with his fact attack. Before long, I was so drunk on facts that I hardly knew what I was saying anymore, but somehow, from the depths of distraction, I managed to have one last go. This time I insisted, in no uncertain terms, that we needed to know the price, that we were busy, which we were, and there was no point in wasting everyone's time if the price wasn't right. This really got under his skin. He looked at me like I was some kind of insolent, ungrateful child and then, slowly and reluctantly, he bent down and pulled a folder out of his briefcase. He started flicking through it impatiently, as I waited in silence, savouring my victory and slowly regaining a sense of coherence. Tanya was looking at me from across the kitchen table, slightly unnerved by the tension that was building up. After a few more minutes, Mr Didier slammed the folder closed and went over to the front window of the kitchen. He pulled a tape from his pocket and measured the length and width.

'It will cost around €1,200', he snapped.

'WHAT?! €1,200 per window?', I gasped.

'Yes, this is the price. It is very good value and a lot less than you will pay for a new window. I can—'.

'That's a crazy price', I interrupted. 'I have already been quoted a price of €650 for a new window.'

The anger and apparent disgust at having to discuss such a distasteful matter as price suddenly spilled over and he started to shout.

'That's not true. How dare you. That's just not true. Nobody has quoted you this kind of price. I'm not a fool.'

'Excuse me, but it is true. I was quoted this price just last week', I responded, raising my voice to match his.

'Who gave you this price?'

'I am not going to argue with you about it. I have a quote for €650 for new windows, so I'm not interested in paying €1,200 for *survitrage*.'

'Where did you get this price? It can only be for some cheap PVC windows.'

'If you must know, it was from Lapeyre [a respected French hardware store], and it was for hardwood windows.'

'Impossible!'

'Look, to be honest I don't really care whether you believe me or not, that's up to you, but this is the price I was quoted and I'm not interested in your *survitrage*, so if you will excuse me, I'm quite busy', I said, opening the door.

He gathered up his things and stormed out the door without saying another word. We later discovered that Mr Didier had in fact already sold *survitrage* to the previous owner, Mrs Sumner, for all the upstairs windows. We counted eighteen windows, which meant that she had probably paid him in excess of €20,000. If we had been living in Ireland we would have reported him to the trading standards agency, but not knowing the system in France we just didn't know where to go or who to contact, and, frankly, we didn't have the time to try to find out.

A few weeks later we had a similar experience with a travelling chimney sweep, who pulled into the yard one day and asked for €600 for cleaning four chimneys. At the time we didn't really know what the going rate was, but we thought it seemed expensive. He then produced a copy of an invoice from the previous year, which showed that Mrs Sumner had paid him €640 for cleaning the same four chimneys. By now I was starting to learn the ropes, so I told him we would pay €400, which he agreed to, but I found out afterwards that the going rate was somewhere between €70 and €80 per chimney, so even at €400 we were still being overcharged.

We eventually found a local company that made and installed new, high-quality hardwood, double-glazed windows for €600 each. We also found a chimney sweep who cleaned all four chimneys for €250. It certainly pays to shop around in rural France, and to avoid, at all costs, a dodgy *survitrage* salesman called Mr Didier.

# 16

# A White Christmas

Christmas was fast approaching, and we had a big decision to make: would we stay or would we go? Since we had first moved abroad, we normally returned to Ireland at Christmas, but in recent years, with two children now in the equation, this was becoming increasingly difficult. The travelling was more complicated, and we seemed to spend most of the holiday period traipsing from one house to another, trying to ensure we spent time with everyone and feeling like we had not spent enough time with anyone. The previous year it had all gotten too much and we all ended up with a really bad dose of the flu, spending the second week of our holidays in bed.

In the end, we decided to stay put for our first year in France, and we weren't disappointed. On Christmas Eve it started to snow, and the following morning the entire countryside had been transformed into a scene from a fairy tale. The soft, white landscape against the deep blue sky was stunning, and it remained like that for the entire week of Christmas.

Christmas morning was spent in front of a big log fire, the kids opening presents while the doting parents indulged in a glass of champagne. Later in the morning, we all went for a walk, built a snowman and then came back to prepare lunch. We had the traditional Irish Christmas lunch, and we even splashed out on an extra-nice bottle of Cahors wine, from our new favourite vineyard, Château Noziéres. Later in the day, we made calls to our two extended families in Ireland and then settled down in front of the television to watch *Elf*. It was probably the calmest and most relaxing Christmas Day we ever had, and thoroughly enjoyable.

The next day, we invited Lars and Helena and some friends of theirs for some of Tanya's special Stephen's Day pie, which consisted of all the leftovers from Christmas lunch covered in a generous layer of mashed potato and baked in the oven. It took us most of the day to work our way through this enormous pie, and then, around 4 p.m., we all set off for a brisk walk through the snow. It was our first family Christmas together in our own house, and it couldn't have been more perfect. It had been a challenging year, but it was ending on a high note.

§

Lying in bed on New Year's morning I found myself reflecting on the past year and wondering what the next twelve months held in store. It frustrated me a little that I still kept comparing our new life in France to our old life in Brussels. I was still looking back, when really I just wanted to look forward. In my heart and soul I knew there was really no point in looking back. This was always something we were going to do. Moving to France had been a dream Tanya and I had for many years. If we had not done it, we would have spent the rest of our lives regretting it or telling ourselves that we were still going to do it, some day.

In some ways the move had been a real success. The children had settled in really well; they were both well on their way to speaking two languages fluently, and we were certain that this was the kind of environment in which we wanted them to grow up. Tanya was also happier: the gîte and B&B had given her a new purpose in life, she had made some good friends, her French was coming on in leaps and bounds, she loved our new home and the area, and she was bubbling with excitement about plans for organic gardening and the rearing of chickens and pigs.

The problem was me. It wasn't that I wanted to go back to Brussels, or to the life we left behind there. I had done all that and I was happy to leave when we did. It was more that I still wasn't living the life I hoped the move would allow me to. The barrier, at least as I saw it, was time, and in particular the amount of it consumed by my day job, and the dependency we still had on this for our income. I could see that we were making progress, which did provide some cause for optimism. We had managed to pay off our mortgage and other outstanding loans and we were getting some income from the gîte and B&B. It was certainly a move in the right direction, but it was still not enough to give us the kind of independence we had hoped for. Provided we kept the overheads to a minimum, I estimated that we needed to at least double this secondary income if we wanted to achieve this kind of independence. Part of the plan for achieving this was to renovate the remainder of the barn, in order to create a second and bigger gîte. I had been working hard to get the funds together for this and I was almost there. I reckoned that if I could stick with it for another year, until all of this was in place, then it looked, on paper at least, like I would finally have the option of scaling back on my day job. It wasn't necessarily that I wanted to quit my job completely, but I certainly wanted to have the option to say 'no' occasionally.

As we started into the New Year I felt more content and reassured about the move and about our new life than I had been for a long time. A lot was going right, and while some things were taking longer to realise than expected, at least we seemed to be going in the right direction.

## Lost in Translation

In mid-January, I had an appointment to go and meet the president of the local chess club. We had met himself and his wife on the village walk, back in November, and they had encouraged us to join the village association and get involved in the many activities they organised – chess, crochet, outings, gourmet events, boules and lots more. It all sounded like a bit of harmless fun, and maybe a chance also to brush up on our French, so we agreed to join. I was particularly interested in the chess, which I had played frequently as a child. When the president heard I was interested he offered to give me a refresher course, which was the purpose of my appointment on this cold, dark, wet winter's evening.

I arrived at the president's house around 8 p.m. and was met at the door by Simona, his wife, a fit and lively octogenarian. She welcomed me with a warm embrace and then proceeded to fuss over me like I was her long-lost son. I was ushered inside and pointed in the direction of a big comfy armchair beside the fire. The president was seated in a similar chair on the other side of the fireplace. He stood up to greet me as Simona rushed off to make tea, as she knew this was 'what English people liked'. Meanwhile, I settled in for a fireside chat with the president. He asked me a few questions about myself and he seemed pleased to learn that I was, in fact, Irish. He was an intelligent man, and he seemed to know quite a lot about Ireland, but he was also curious to know more. A short while later, Simona arrived with some Earl Grey tea and two plates of cakes and biscuits. She proceeded to sit on the arm of the president's chair while we continued chatting about Ireland and about life in France, and Simona even gave me a few tips on gardening and pest control.

An hour later, there still hadn't been any mention of chess and it was getting late, so I asked the president if he would like to have a game. However, the president decided that it was best to start with an explanation of the rules. I insisted that I had a reasonably good idea of the rules and that it would probably all come back to me once we started to play, but my protestations fell on deaf ears and he continued on unperturbed. Twenty minutes later, I was up to speed on the rules: the ones I already knew, and what seemed to be a few extra ones thrown in by the president. And then, finally, the game kicked off – the master and his 'young' apprentice. The opening moves were tense. The president barely blinked an eye as he slowly and meticulously moved his pawns down the board, each move taking at least four to five minutes. It was now well past 10 p.m. and I was keen to get home, so I moved my first pawn out two spaces. The president was not impressed. This was against the rules; I would have to go back and start again. It was certainly a rule when I played all those years earlier, but I wasn't going to argue with the president of the chess club.

We played on at a snail's pace, with the president regularly interjecting to explain why he made a particular move, or to critically analyse my moves and point out how and why he would have done it differently. It went on like this for quite a while, the wily old master patiently guiding and instructing his young student. But then something happened that really wasn't meant to happen. Somehow, either by accident or good fortune, I managed to put the president's king in check. It was all over.

The room fell into silence and it felt like I had slain the president himself. For two or three minutes he didn't speak. He just stared at the board, in shock. He then called Simona and told her that he 'might have' lost; he asked her to have a look to see if he had missed something. The poor man, he was gutted. It wasn't supposed to end like this. We eventually agreed that it was just a fluke, beginner's luck or whatever you want to call it, and so the president demanded that we line the pieces up again.

He regained his composure and, just as before, he continued to instruct and advise me on the finer points of the game, even as I continued to explain that I had played chess before. As the game progressed, I started to get the upper hand again and I could see that the president was getting agitated. I don't know what it was; it seemed like the more I wasn't supposed to win the greater that likelihood actually became. The president was a much better player and on any other day he would have beaten me every time, but today it was somehow preordained that I was to be the victor, and it was landing me in a spot of bother. A short while later I won the second game. I tried to soften the blow by telling the president that he had taught me too well, but he remained transfixed. A few minutes later he whispered something to Simona. I asked her if everything was okay, and she replied that the president thought I wasn't telling them everything; that I must have played before. I tried to explain that I had been trying to tell them that all evening, that my poor French must have let me down, but it didn't seem to wash. They looked at me suspiciously, as I insisted again that it was just luck, which it was, and that the president's 'tips' had really helped me and I still had much to learn from him. That seemed to help, and the president perked up a little, but I had to refuse the offer of a third game, not just on the grounds that there would be a definite falling out if I beat him again, but also because it was late and I really had to get home.

Before I left, I asked about the club, which was due to meet the next day. Simona told me that they would meet around 2 p.m., which surprised me, as I assumed a club like this would meet in the evening. But of course most, if not all, of the members were retired and for them it was a nice way to pass the afternoon, in the company of friends and neighbours. The president suggested to Simona that they would put me up against Marcus. This stopped her in her tracks.

'Marcus? But he's very …'.

'No, I think he's ready', said the president, with a proud look on his face. Marcus was also retired, but younger than Simona and the president, probably in his mid-sixties. He had moved to France from Switzerland in his twenties and married a local French girl. I was told he was a dab hand at the chess. But there was a problem – I had a job, and I was already taking Friday afternoons off for art classes. I just couldn't take Tuesday afternoons off as well. I explained this to Simona and the president. They looked disappointed, bitterly disappointed in fact. They had just found and 'trained' a potential new chess champion and now he was telling them he couldn't play, because he had to work.

I didn't show up at the club the following day. It might have looked like I chickened out of the showdown with Marcus, but far from it. I was actually relishing the tête-à-tête with the canny Swiss but, unfortunately, on this occasion making a living had to take precedence. Tanya did go along, and she reported the high jinks of the afternoon to me later that evening: crochet and knitting for the ladies, mostly of a certain age, while the men battled it out on the chess board.

The experience really brought it home to us that we were living in an area with a very different demographic to anywhere we had lived before. There were very few people our age in the commune. Most of the local residents were retired, and because of this most of the local services and activities were geared towards this older age group. This was something we could live with, but it was another unforeseen aspect of life in rural France that we had to adjust to. In the ideal world, we would have preferred if there had been art classes and chess in the evening, with perhaps one or two people a little closer in age to ourselves, but we don't live in an ideal world. As in most places people live, there are upsides and downsides. We live in a beautiful, quiet, peaceful area, but the reason it is like this is because it has practically no industry, few jobs, and, therefore, a small and older population.

# 17

# A Man Needs a Tractor

I realised pretty soon after we arrived in France that sooner or later we would need to invest in a tractor. It wasn't urgent and I knew it would be costly so it went on the long finger, but by February the time had come. Some people, including Tanya, might have thought this was some kind of male self-indulgence, a mid-life crisis or a boy's toy, but I knew better than to get drawn into that one – we did have 40 acres after all. By the end of February we had burnt all the wood that Mrs Sumner had left behind, and our beautiful green pastures were being overrun with bushes and scrub. I convinced myself, and Tanya, that we needed a tractor and trailer to collect wood and a topper to keep the fields in check. And so the decision was made to press ahead with these lofty acquisitions.

As a child growing up on a farm in Ireland in the 1970s I developed a great love for the Massey Ferguson (MF) 135. Like many farm kids back then, and probably now as well, I was driving tractors not too long after I learned to walk, and the MF 135 was my favourite. It was small, so a better size for a child, and it just looked the real deal – an iconic tractor. So, if I was going to buy a tractor, then it just had to be an

MF 135. For some months I had already been keeping an eye out for one – checking the small ads online, so when the time came, I had a few possibilities lined up.

The first was on a farm in the Dordogne, about an hour's drive away. It was a dull wet Saturday morning when we set off to have a look. We pulled into the farmyard and met Julian, a friendly, easy-going man of about fifty, who took me and Ned through to an old hay barn and into a shed at the rear of the farm. There were two tractors there: an MF 135 and a bigger tractor, an International. Both were for sale. Julian explained that his father had recently passed away and he was changing the two older models for a bigger, newer tractor. I think it's called progress, but there was something about this modernisation business that I found upsetting. I wanted more than ever to give a new life to the MF 135. But there were a few problems to overcome: it didn't start too easily, and, on top of that, the brakes were sticking. Julian assured me that it was a good tractor and that these problems could be easily sorted out, but I wasn't so sure. After a short test drive, he brought us into the farmhouse to see the papers.

It was a charming old country house and in the kitchen Julian's mother was sitting at the table, near a big range cooker. She was elderly but warm and friendly. She reminded me of my own grandmother in Ireland: offering us drinks and cake and biscuits, and fussing over Ned, just like my own grandmother had fussed over me when I was his age. As she moved slowly around the kitchen, collecting plates and glasses, she quizzed me about life and farming in Ireland, standing still every so often to listen attentively to my responses. I told her about my childhood memories of growing up on a farm: the small fields bordered by stone walls; my memories of my grand-uncles working the fields with horses (still not uncommon in 1970s Ireland); and how rapidly things had changed after Ireland joined the European Economic Community, as it was then known. She hung on every word and as I spoke a tear trickled down her face. She clearly recognised something familiar in this Ireland of my youth, which had now largely disappeared. Sitting there in her kitchen, I understood and felt this connection. It was strange but I felt at home, safe, like I was among my own kind of people. Julian's mother told me of how her late husband would have loved to meet us, how he loved Ireland and had always wanted to go there.

We didn't buy the tractor that day, but it was an encounter I won't forget for a while. It reminded me of how much more at home I always felt with country and farming people. It also reminded me of the Ireland in which I grew up and which I had a strong attachment to, and the similarities between that Ireland and this part of rural France gave me a feeling of being in a place that was somehow familiar.

The search for a tractor continued, and the following day I came across the advertisement I had been waiting for: 'MF 135 for sale in the Lot, asking price: €3,500'. From the photos it looked like a bit of a wreck, but on the plus side it was the right tractor, in the right place and at the right price, so I arranged a viewing for that afternoon. Around 3 p.m. we loaded up and set off on the forty-minute drive to Cézac, a small village just south of Cahors. When we finally arrived at the farm, which was located at the end of long, winding lane, we spotted a tractor and hay turner parked in the farmyard.

'Is that it?', said Tanya, looking aghast.

'Yes, I think so. Do you not like it?'

'Well, it's a bit dingy looking isn't it? And does it really need that twine to hold it together?'

She was right; it really did look like a pile of scrap.

We parked a little further on and I got out, alone, to meet the seller. His name was Gaston and he couldn't have been more than nineteen or twenty, but he was chatty and had the air of someone who was well used to selling things. He assured me it was a gem of a little tractor. 'Impeccable', was the word he used. But it wasn't obvious from looking at it that it was such a show stopper, so I didn't reach immediately for my cheque book. Gaston continued to sing its praises, however. I think he probably assumed from the look of me that I knew very little about tractors, and he wasn't too far off.

However he needn't have bothered with his marketing spiel. All he had to do was to start the engine and the rest was a foregone conclusion. As soon as I heard the sound of the Perkins three-cylinder engine I actually got emotional. I had to turn away for fear that Gaston might see my eyes welling up and seize the opportunity to hike the price up another grand. It was strange; I didn't think a tractor would affect me that way, but the sound of the MF 135 engine is so distinctive and it instantly reconnected me with a very happy time in my life. Gaston probably knew the game was up at this stage, but he offered me a spin on it anyway, just to drive home his advantage. I drove to the far side of the field, glad of the chance to have a few moments alone to regain my composure. Sure enough, it had seen better days: the gears were tight, the mud guards were rattling and the steering was so tight I nearly broke my arms trying to negotiate it through the muddy terrain. In fact, to get back to base I had to resort to using the brakes to manoeuvre it, a bit like a tank.

'Impeccable', said Gaston, as I ground to a halt beside him.

'Not quite', I said, deciding it was time to assert my chronological advantage.

'There are a few problems with the brakes, the gears are very stiff, the lights don't work, the mud guards are loose … I'll give you €2,500.'

He looked at me a bit weirdly, realising that he might have misread me.

'No, no, I can't do it. €3,000 is the absolute limit. It's a very good tractor; impeccable.'

'I'll tell you what; I'll give you €3,000 if you throw in that trailer over there and deliver the two to my place.'

'Impeccable', said Gaston, looking like a man who would have thrown in his mother and father if the price had been right. We shook hands and I gave him €1,000 on the spot, with the rest to be paid on delivery. He said he would drive it to our place the next day. I said nothing, but I wondered if he realised what he was taking on – a 40-kilometre trip on a vintage tractor, with no brakes, no lights and stiff gears, towing a trailer that would have looked more at home behind a team of donkeys.

I went back to the car and told Tanya that I had bought the tractor and the medieval trailer that I pointed out in a nearby shed. I knew that she wanted to be happy for me and I could see that she was trying hard to smile, but behind the façade I sensed concern. Not so much about the tractor and trailer, but about the fact that her husband was turning into some kind of two-bit farmer. What would it be next, baler twine to hold up my trousers? As we drove out the gate and I glanced back at my new acquisitions, I must admit I had the same feeling myself. I broke out in a cold sweat and was immediately overcome by a powerful sense of buyer's remorse. Had I really just paid €3,000 for those two museum pieces? Gaston really saw me coming.

It's a weird thing, but I could linger for hours in a supermarket, trying to find a good deal on a chicken or a bottle of wine, but when it came to transactions costing thousands of Euro, I always seem to make snap decisions and then I start analysing them afterwards. When I got home I phoned my brother in Ireland, looking for reassurance. I had already sent him the photos of the tractor and he had given me a few tips on how to test it, but now it was time for the post-purchase assessment.

'You didn't buy that heap of dirt did you?', came the response on the other end of the phone. Not quite the feedback I was looking for, but there was a brutal honesty to it that only a brother could get away with. Probably sensing my disappointment, he later softened his tone, and by the end of the conversation he was raving about what a great buy it was, insisting that you wouldn't get anything like it in Ireland for less than €5,000. That's older brothers for you.

The next day, Gaston and his father arrived with the merchandise. The father seemed a bit impatient, like he didn't want any hand, act or part in his son's dealing with this crazy Irish guy who was into buying clapped-out tractors. When they had everything offloaded, including two extra back wheels for the tractor, which looked like they had been ripped asunder by wild dogs, I paid Gaston the balance and they were gone.

'*Au revoir*', I said as they pulled away, with the father looking at Gaston as if he was a major disappointment. Maybe he had higher hopes for his son, but he seemed like a pretty sharp cookie to me, so I really didn't know what the problem was.

After they had left, I moved the tractor and trailer around the back of the house, out of sight, in order to give myself some time to come to terms with the fact that they were now ours. Maybe I would feel better about the whole thing the next day, I thought. As I strolled back to the house, my head down deep in thought, I spotted something near the edge of the garden that looked like a dead bird. When I got closer I discovered that it was in fact a dead owl. It was such a beautiful bird, with its white and gold plumage and almost human-like face. I called Tanya, who was at the other side of the garden. I tried to signal to her not to bring the children, but they followed her anyway.

I dug a hole and Tanya and the children looked on as I buried the owl and covered the body with stones and earth. I expected the kids to be upset by this but in fact they were quite stoical, and more interested in asking questions about what had happened to the owl and why I was burying it. This was something we noticed about the children's reaction to life and death in the country – they generally accepted things as they were presented to them.

Tanya and I were probably more saddened by the sight of the dead owl, and we wondered if that was the beginning of the end of the owls, which Mrs Sumner said had been living in the upper part of the west tower for over twenty years. With one of the partners dead, what would now become of the other, we wondered. That night we sat outside in the garden to see if there was any activity in the tower. It was just past 7 p.m., the time when one of the owls would normally leave the nest to go in search of food. But on this occasion, there was no sign of life and not a sound. By 7.45 p.m. I was ready to give up. It was getting cold, it was almost dark and I really didn't think we were going to see anything. However, Tanya persuaded me to stay for another five minutes. A few seconds later, our long vigil was finally rewarded. As we looked up in the fading light, a small white figure emerged through the opening in the tower and stood, forlornly surveying the surroundings, her head moving from right to left and then back again. I don't know why, but we just assumed that this was a female and the dead bird was male. At first we thought that she might have been looking out for her partner, to see if he was coming back. It was quite sad seeing her there all alone.

What would she do now? Would she leave the tower? Would she survive without the companionship of her partner? We looked on as she gazed into the distance. Tanya began to sob, and then the owl looked down at us, holding her gaze for several seconds. She lifted her head again, looked left and right once more, and then flew across to the opposite tower. She stood there for a few minutes, looking back in the direction from which she came. This was unusual. Normally the owls just flew out through the opening and onwards to the surrounding woods and fields. What was she waiting for, and why was she looking back at the other tower? Was it a last goodbye, before she left the home she had shared with her partner for good?

Just then, another small, white figure emerged from the tower, and stood momentarily in the opening, just as the first owl had done, before also flying across to the opposite tower. Tanya's tears were now giving way to a tearful smile, as it seemed like the couple were still together. But before we had time to really process what we had just seen, another owl emerged, and then another and then another and, after a short pause, a sixth owl stepped forward and then joined the others on the opposite ledge.

We could hardly believe our eyes. It was a relief to know that the first owl wasn't alone, but the fact that there was now a whole family of owls in the tower was really amazing. As we watched what we assumed to be the parent leading its offspring on possibly their first nocturnal sortie in the woods, we felt reassured that we would have owls in our tower for some time to come. We still hadn't solved the mystery of the dead bird, but it was probably one of the young ones, which may have hit the electricity cable that ran along the road beside our garden. It seems that this is common among young birds learning to fly.

It had been another day of highs and lows, which was now an established feature of our life in France: weighed down by the demands of the move and the burdens of the unknown and the unforeseen one moment, and jumping for joy, excited about some new discovery or new encounter the next. But it was the anticipation of these high points, these special moments, that carried us through the more challenging times and made it all worthwhile.

# 18

# *Take Two*

As winter gave way to spring, we moved into our second year in the Lot. With the experience we had gained during the first year, life began to get a little easier, and we were now feeling better equipped for life in rural France. But despite this there were still challenges, and our determination to make a success of our new life continued to be tested.

In June we went to the evening market in Lherm, another one of the Lot's beautiful medieval villages. Several rows of long tables were laid out, with friends, neighbours and tourists barbequing locally produced food and enjoying each other's company until late into the evening. Unfortunately for us, however, we ended up sitting alone at one of these long tables, not really knowing anyone else there, and not speaking French well enough to thrust ourselves on complete strangers. It was a beautiful summer's evening, the food was great, there was some nice music playing and if we had had some people to share it with it would have been perfect. But we didn't, and it felt like we were alone, apart from the crowd and apart from the fun.

As we sat at our table, observing all that was going on around us, I wondered if we would ever really feel at home in France, or would we always be slightly on the margins, never quite sure of our place. What probably made it worse was the fact that all my family at home were going to my cousin's fortieth birthday party that weekend. It was going to be a big party, and I really would have liked to have been there. I loved these family occasions: it was always good fun and a good chance to strengthen close family bonds. I missed that.

A few days after the market in Lherm I also got some bad news from home. It was Father's Day in France, and I was being treated to a lie-on and a late breakfast in bed, but I was only minutes into this little indulgence when Tanya came into the room with the telephone.

'It's Fiona', she said, in a sombre voice, 'your dad's in hospital.'

I could feel my body tense up as I grabbed the phone.

'Hi Fiona, what's wrong?'

'Daddy's had some kind of turn …'.

Time stands still when you hear news like this, and I hung on her every word as she explained what had happened. Fortunately, he had since stabilised, but the doctors still didn't know what the problem was. This is the worst kind of news to get when you live abroad. It triggers all kinds of feelings and emotions: regret (for not being there), helplessness (for not being able to do anything), worry (as you can't really see for yourself what's going on) and even loneliness (as you don't have the support of other members of your family or the other people closely involved).

This news also meant that my parents' planned visit a few weeks later was now on hold, which was also disappointing as we had been looking forward to seeing them. We didn't tell the children the details of what was going on but later that day we booked flights to go home ourselves. In the evening, I told Ned and Astrid that my parents had decided not to come out to visit but that we were now going to go home instead. They both loved Ireland, so this was great news for them, and it's funny how the happiness of kids can rub off on you, even when you're at your lowest. A few minutes later we were enthusiastically counting the number of days (or 'sleeps' as they put it) until we were going home, and when we got to the end we all rolled back on Ned's bed and sang in unison, 'ten more days to Ireland, yeah!'

By the time we got home, my father was much better than I had expected. He was out of hospital and, while he wasn't 100 per cent, he was in good spirits, and I was glad to be able to see this firsthand. The weather in Ireland was also unusually good, so it turned out to be quite a pleasant trip. It was great to see our families again and to see that my father was recovering well. We returned to France feeling a little lighter and ready for what we hoped would be another busy summer, and if the weather had been good in Ireland then it was exceptional in France. For the rest of the summer you could have counted on one hand the amount of times it rained, which was great in one way but also slightly unnerving, especially when the temperature topped 40 degrees Celsius, as it did a few times in August.

A byproduct of the hot, dry weather was the invasion of our garden by wild animals, presumably in search of green vegetation, which could only be found in places where there was some kind of irrigation system. There were snakes aplenty, including one very portly fellow who became a frequent visitor to our terrace. We were assured by neighbours that the snakes in the Lot were harmless but we still didn't get too close, just in case. Then there were the moles that kept pushing up piles of earth everywhere, the crane that came fishing in our pond, the fox that regularly crossed our driveway and, best of all, another clutch of baby owls.

In amongst all these wonderful wild creatures, there were also two youngsters of the human variety, who were growing in stature and in confidence every day, and who seemed perfectly at home in this natural environment. A particular joy during this second year was to hear the children speaking

French. It had taken them a few months to develop the confidence to speak uninhibited in social settings, but by the second year they had mastered it and they spoke with such perfect intonation that it was impossible to tell the difference from the local French children. Listening to them in conversation with their friends we soon realised that, even though we were Irish parents, we were in fact rearing two French children – a further incentive, if we needed one, to improve our own language skills.

In July, we celebrated Ned's fifth birthday. A few days after his party we rented a campervan and drove down to the Mediterranean to meet my sister and her family at Argelès-sur-Mer. This gave us a chance to catch up with some of what was going on back in Ireland. Mostly it was bad news: the recession and the crash in the property market were affecting most people in some way, my sister and her husband included. He was a builder by trade and was finding it almost impossible to get work. It had gotten to the stage where they were contemplating emigrating. I had been keeping in touch with the news in Ireland so I knew all the headline stories, but it doesn't really sink in until you hear how this impacts on the lives of real people, people you know and love.

Living in rural France, we were insulated from the worst effects of this particular crisis, but Ireland had been there before, and I had firsthand experience of what it was like then. When I graduated from university in 1989, unemployment was at an all-time high of 17.5 per cent, there were almost no job opportunities, and the outlook for young graduates like myself was bleaker than bleak. Emigration was the only real option for most young people. I stayed, because at the time I was determined to make a life for myself in Ireland, where all my family and friends were, but I paid a price – unemployment and insecure temporary work do nothing for your self-esteem. But I muddled through and eventually I went back to university and got a postgraduate qualification in business studies, which opened up other doors, including the opportunity to set up a microbrewery, which I did with my brother in 1996. By this time, things had begun to improve in Ireland. We were already in the early days of the Celtic Tiger and jobs and money were becoming more plentiful, but recessions leave their imprint; they shape who you are and become part of your character. One important lesson I learned from this experience was to never give up hope – things never stay the same, and if you keep getting up in the morning, keep yourself busy and try to stay positive your luck will eventually turn. It was for this reason that I was confident that, in time, Ireland would pull through its most recent crisis, just as it did before, but this was no consolation for my brother-in-law. However, he seemed to be handling it well and I think he enjoyed the holiday, as we all did.

§

When we got back from Argelès-sur-Mer we had a request for a winter booking in the gîte, which was a pleasant surprise, as we hadn't anticipated any bookings outside of the summer season. If it worked out, it would really boost the income potential of the gîte and inch us even closer to that elusive figure we needed to hit for financial independence. In financial terms, it did actually work out. The only issue was the tenant, Jane, an Englishwoman in her mid-forties, who was escaping a 'messy' divorce in the UK. She wasn't a problematic tenant in the conventional sense – she paid her rent and generally kept the place clean and tidy. The problem was that she was clearly traumatised by the whole divorce business and desperately in need of some kind of counselling. Unfortunately, in the absence of such professional help, Tanya and I found ourselves on the front line. With me, she spent quite a bit of time denigrating men, insisting that she didn't want to have anything to do with the opposite sex for a very long time; she said she had enough of men and craved a quiet, solitary life. Being a man myself, it left me feeling a little uneasy, like I was being continually told to get lost. Tanya, on the other hand, became her confidante, and before too long Jane was spending long hours in our kitchen, sharing some quite personal details of her life and seeking Tanya's advice on various aspects of her divorce. Basically, she needed someone to talk to and by default that person became Tanya. But it was difficult: Tanya had other work to do and didn't feel qualified to give the kind of support and advice that Jane was looking for and needed. In the end, it became quite a strain and I don't think she was too disappointed when Jane finally left.

Her leaving was quite sudden. She had been staying with us for about six months at the time and then, one day, without warning, she was gone. We had a call from her a few days later to say she was back on the UK. She had packed her things before she left and now she wanted us to put them in storage, so she could pick them up when she came back, supposedly at the end of the month. It was March at this stage and she had been renting the gîte since the previous October. We put her bags in our basement, ready for collection, but she never showed up at the end of the month and, as I write now, almost three years later, they're still there.

From talking to other expat neighbours and friends, many of whom have lived in the Lot for a number of years, we discovered that this kind of winter booking was not so uncommon. It seems that many people take advantage of the lower rents in winter to escape to France for a few months, which seems like a good idea, and probably is in a lot of cases, but some people also underestimate the challenges involved. The south of France in winter time is very different to what it is in summer. Besides the cold weather, there are far fewer people around and it can be a lonely and unwelcoming place if you don't have some kind of support network in place. This is even more important if you have problems in your life that you are trying to overcome, as you can be pretty sure that these problems will follow you no matter where you go.

# 19

# Taking Stock

Towards the end of our second year in France it felt like a good time to take stock. Not everything had gone to plan. There had been some unpleasant surprises, some frustrations and a few disappointments, but despite this, a lot had gone right. Firstly, we were really glad to be living in the countryside again, and to have finally satisfied a long-held curiosity about what it would be like to live in France. It was not the easy, carefree existence that we might have imagined: we still had children to rear, bills to pay, and work and business commitments to take care of, but as a family we were spending more time together, even if it often involved work of some kind, and we were also spending a lot more time outdoors.

So, two years on, I had no doubt in my mind that the move was the right thing at the right time, but I still couldn't say it was mission accomplished. For me personally, the biggest challenge was breaking old habits, especially in relation to work. Interestingly, it was around this time that I met and struck up a conversation with a Frenchman on the train to Paris one day. We got talking about jobs and careers, and he caught me slightly off-guard when he said he didn't have a job. He looked respectable, and sounded intelligent and well-informed, so I was pretty sure he wasn't some kind of layabout, but I wasn't sure how I should greet this revelation. He explained that he had packed in his job in public transport and was now pursuing his 'passions' on a full-time basis. He was married but had no children, and he estimated that he had saved enough money to keep himself going for about ten years. Beyond that? Well, he didn't really know, but he didn't seem too concerned. Anyway, he was already starting to earn some money from his passions so it was possible that his savings would last longer than ten years, maybe indefinitely. His passions were painting, photography and fishing, and he had managed to combine all three by specialising in paintings and photographs with a fishing or maritime theme. In fact, he was just on his way back from a small village on the Mediterranean, where he had been commissioned by a wealthy tycoon to paint a picture of his wooden schooner.

It was the first time in many years that I had met someone who had made such a bold life change and I was intrigued, even more so because he seemed so at ease with himself. This is what I wanted to do. I wanted to be able to take this kind of bold step. However, later, as I sat alone in a hotel room in Brussels, I wondered if I was ready. It sounded great in theory, but in practice I was afraid, of two things in particular: firstly, would we have money worries? The income from the gîtes and B&B, and some other investments, was probably enough to live on, but it was a close shave. It certainly wouldn't be a life of luxury and I was concerned that I might be depriving Tanya and the children in some way. My second concern was more to do with my own sense of who I was: would I be able to make a success of any of my 'passions'? Would I ever, seriously, be able to call myself a writer, for example, and, if not, what would I be and how would I feel about myself?

So, after two years in France, I still couldn't say I had fully made the transition I set out to make, but I was okay with that. It was a work in progress, and I think this was the best way to describe where we were in terms of the move overall. Things are never perfect. There are always challenges no matter where you live. The secret, I was learning, was to recognise and accept this, and, once you do, your expectations become more realistic and you automatically find yourself better able to enjoy the good things, the things you managed to get right.

## What I Know Now

When I started to write this book, I wanted to document the real-life experiences of our move to France and to provide some insights for people who might be considering doing something similar. I always knew we weren't the only ones who dreamed of such a move but, I have to say, from the moment we actually went public with our plans I was amazed by the number of people who confided in me about their secret plans or desires to do the same. I would say that this was probably more than half of the people I knew in the thirty-five-to-fifty age category.

My advice to anyone in this situation is to think long and hard before doing anything rash. Be clear about why you are moving, what you want to achieve and what kind of location you need to make this a reality. Moving country or moving from the city to the countryside is not going to meet your every expectation and, if you are not properly prepared, it might not meet any of them.

Having already set out on this journey, it is obvious to me now that are there some essential ingredients for a successful move which should not be ignored. Firstly, learn the local language. Even if you don't attain fluency, try to have a reasonable grasp of the language before you move. By this I mean you should be able to understand people who make an effort to speak to you slowly and clearly, and be able to hold a basic conversation. This will help you to integrate and to negotiate officialdom, and, importantly, will provide a basis to further improve your language skills once you are in situ.

Secondly, don't give yourself financial headaches. Be sure you have enough money for the move and for any renovations or other work you need to undertake. Get quotes from local people and allow for contingencies, as they always materialise. On top of this, you need to know where your ongoing income is going to come from, and be realistic – not only in terms of your income estimates, but also in calculating what you will need to live on. Once you have identified where the initial investment is going to come from, and your source or sources of ongoing income, you're pretty much sorted, right? Wrong. Chances are you have still underestimated the investment needed and overestimated your earning capacity, so you need a contingency, a back-up plan in case, as is likely, things don't turn out as you expect. Our contingency was the possibility of me being able to work from home, so at least we had a fall-back position when the renovation costs escalated and when it took longer than expected to get the gîte business up and running. But this was not part of the master plan. I was supposed to scale back my work. Looking back now I can see that we probably over-invested in living space and under-invested in income-generating space and, because of this, attaining our financial goals was set back by at least three to four years. If I hadn't had a job I could carry on from home, then our plans would have been in disarray.

And so my third ingredient for success is to think long and hard about what kind of property you need. You will obviously have some essential requirements, but also certain desirable but non-essential criteria. Identify these and be sure you know the difference between the two, as it is almost impossible to find the absolute dream property, so you will need some inbuilt flexibility. If the property that catches your eye includes some of your non-essential features, or if, as is often the case, it includes features that you hadn't even considered, be careful. Additional land or a bigger house than you expected seems great in principle, but in practice you need to think through the implications of this. What will it mean in terms of the additional workload to maintain the land or the additional rooms, or what additional costs will you incur for heating or fencing or other ongoing costs? You may find that these additional features are more trouble than they're worth.

If it's possible, my advice would be to rent before you buy. It is very difficult to property search when you don't live in the area you plan to move to. Mostly, you're restricted to looking at websites, which often only advertise the properties that are more difficult to shift. The real gems are snapped up quickly and never make it to the websites, so if you are on the ground and keeping your eyes open you can greatly enhance your chances of finding what you are looking for.

Fourthly, think carefully about where you want to live. If you want to live by the coast then you should not be property hunting in the Dordogne or the Auvergne. Choose your region carefully, taking account of your budget, interests, goals and expectations, especially in terms of climate. Once you have decided on a region or regions, think long and hard about the kind of locality you are looking for. Many people are looking for something within walking distance of a village (but not in the village) where there is a bakery and a café, and near enough to a larger town or city, with supermarkets and other services. If this is what you are looking for, remember there are only so many such places in France and you may not find something that meets all of your other criteria in such a location. We found a nice house, within walking distance of a village, and near a big town with supermarkets and all other essential services, but there is no bakery or café in our village. It was a compromise we would have preferred not to have had to make but we had to do it, so you have to be prepared, and know your limits.

If you haven't adequately addressed each of these issues, my advice would be don't move to France. The highways and byways of rural France are littered with the shattered dreams of overzealous expats who misjudged, miscalculated or never really considered the complexities of living in a foreign country. If the fundamentals are right – if your relationship is strong and if you have enough money and decent language skills – you have a good chance of succeeding. If not, well, let's just say your chances are somewhat diminished. If things do stack up, it's important that you don't prevaricate too long. Educate yourself, do the research and then make a decision; don't wait forever, trying to ensure everything is perfect. There will always be some level of risk and you have to accept this and embrace it.

Ultimately, you have to trust and have confidence in your resourcefulness to overcome the unforeseen or to deal with the normal day-to-day challenges. If you are someone who is resilient and you have the staying power to overcome difficult challenges then you will eventually come out on top, as you have probably already done on many other occasions.

*Epilogue*

It's now four years since we moved and I'm happy to report that we are still living in France. They say it takes around five years to properly settle in to a new community and I think there is a lot of truth in this. With every passing year we get to know our local friends and neighbours a little better, a familiarity develops and with it a sense of belonging, of being part of a community. When I'm away now and I return to our little corner of France it really feels like I'm coming home. This is my place, I know it intimately: the people, the landscape, and the way things work, or don't work. We are now a part of it. But this didn't happen by accident. It's not automatic. We have worked hard at making a new life here and now, finally, it seems to be paying dividends. This last year especially our efforts to integrate took a big step forward when we initiated and helped to set up a local community café.

Initially, our motivation for getting involved in this was the fact that we missed having something equivalent to a local pub in Ireland – somewhere to meet people and have a drink or a coffee. So at the end of last summer, Tanya and I put out some feelers to see if some of our neighbours might also be interested. We quickly had the support of three French neighbours and the five of us then set about developing the idea, eventually creating an association and securing the use of the local *foyer rurale* (community hall).

In April 2014 the café opened its doors to the public. Over 100 people turned up for the opening night, mostly from our own and a few neighbouring communes. We were amazed with this turnout and with the outpouring of support for our little project. Over 70 people joined the association on the first night and many of them are now actively helping out in what is a purely voluntary initiative. For the moment, the café only opens two nights per month but this is already helping to recreate a dynamic that had not existed in the community for a very long time. People are meeting more often and an ongoing programme of activities ensures there is something of interest to everyone, including children.

Beyond the wider benefits to the community, however, this project has also had a major impact on our lives. Not only do we have somewhere nearby where we can go for a drink and relax, but, more importantly, we now also have a role in the community. We are actively contributing to the running of an important new local amenity, which means we are meeting and working together with local people on a regular basis. This has made an enormous difference to our lives. Within the last twelve months we have moved from the fringes closer to the heart of the community and this is a nice feeling. It's even helping to improve our French. On the opening night of the café Tanya and I both gave speeches in French, something we would have never considered possible even a few months earlier.

In parallel with our efforts to better integrate, we have also continued to develop our gîte and B&B business; in 2013 we completed the renovations on another large section of the barn, creating a second, two-bedroomed gîte, so effectively trebling our capacity. Bookings for both gîtes continue to be good, ahead of our original expectations. The B&B business has been less successful, which is partly due to a lower demand for this kind of accommodation, especially without the possibility of evening meals, but also partly due to the fact that we haven't really pushed it in terms of promotion.

Having people stay in your home, even though for us it is a separate part of the house, can feel like an intrusion sometimes, especially when you have young children. You find yourself fretting about the noise they make or the toys they leave in the guests' breakfast area, and generally it's more difficult to relax in the house when you are sharing it with paying guests. For this reason, we are happy that the business is occasional rather than continual, with a notable increase in the peak period of July and August.

We have also managed to find a good, reliable builder. Not an easy task by any means, but after much trial and error we have, for now at least, found someone who shows up when he says he will, does what you agree with him, and doesn't try to extort more than the amount agreed. And he's also a nice guy, but I won't be divulging his details. This is one revelation I would like to keep to myself.

When I took stock of our situation at the end of our second year in France I identified myself and my work–life imbalance as one of the main unresolved issues. Well, this is still an issue, as I am one of these people who can't sit still for very long, but I have made progress. My main objective was to achieve a greater balance between work, family and personal interests and, although there are times when one or other still dominates (usually work), the overall balance is significantly better now than before we moved. As a family we eat breakfast together every morning, Tanya and I are both there when the children get home from school, we have dinner together every evening, and we spend most Sundays together, hiking, watching films, playing football, going to markets or just relaxing at home.

In terms of work, I'm also concentrating more now on the things I want to do. I am getting more involved in projects dealing with climate change and sustainability, something I feel strongly about, and this recently led to my involvement in the setting up of a European network called ECOLISE. Sandwiched in between work and family, there has also been some room for writing and I hope this will continue to develop in the future.

So, while we won't be getting too smug about it, I think we have achieved much of what we set out to achieve. It has taken longer than expected, we have had to work harder than expected, and it is different to what we expected, but it has been incredibly worthwhile and an amazing learning experience. Living in the south of France is not the romantic existence that we imagined. Certainly there is romance, which initially at least was the magnet that kept us here, but it's an impure romance – tainted by the imperfections of the real world in which we all live. This is what makes it challenging but also rewarding, as you learn to cope, adjust and surmount the obstacles that present themselves.

We started this journey with the intention of realising a dream, but what I have realised is that a dream is just that – a dream. And it remains a dream, even after you've 'succeeded', because there are always sacrifices or compromises to be made, so there is always something to strive for; you never reach perfection. The secret, perhaps, is to learn to be happy that you have realised part of your dream, and not to become preoccupied with the parts you haven't, especially in the early days, when the temptation is to strive to create the utopia you had imagined in your mind's eye. This is a mistake, and it can cause frustration and distract from the possibility of enjoying those aspects of your life that are exactly as you want them to be. Living the dream is a fantasy. Almost living the dream is eminently more attainable, and by far a more realistic goal.

Then again, as I sit in the shade on the terrace, sipping a pre-dinner glass of rosé, and feasting my eyes on a semi-wild landscape of forest and pasture, illuminated by the evening sun, it strikes me that maybe sometimes we just analyse things too much.

A bientôt!